CLUB EVEREST

FAVORITE SPANISH DISHES

FAVORITE SPANISH DISHES

EDITORIAL EVEREST, S. A.

MADRID • LEON • BARCELONA • SEVILLA • GRANADA • VALENCIA
ZARAGOZA • BILBAO • LAS PALMAS DE GRAN CANARIA • LA CORUÑA
PALMA DE MALLORCA •ALICANTE — MEXICO • BUENOS AIRES

Translated by: Mr. and Mrs. Gonzalez

Foto Portada: SALMER

QUINTA EDICION

ISBN 84-241-2824 — 9
Depósito legal: LE-1041 — 1987

EDITORIAL EVERGRÁFICAS, S. A. — Ctra. León-La Coruña, km 5
LEÓN (España)

CONTENTS

Introduction

Every year thousands of turists return to their homes with pleasant memories of the Spanish sunshine, «flamenco» dancers, bullfights, fiestas, etc., and a special remembrance of the delicious Spanish food they have enjoyed.

For this reason we bring this book to you with favorite Spanish dishes so that you may reproduce these dishes in your home.

Although each recipe is given a particular title, there are variations of them as each region in Spain has its favorite version.

Other authors abuse the usage of Spanish words when giving the recipe a title, to make the dish appear more authentic. We have tried to eliminate this due to the variations in different regions as mentioned above.

We hope that you will enjoy preparing the dishes for your family and friends as much as we have enjoyed preparing them for you. If so, our purpose will have been fulfilled.

Aperitives and hors d'oeuvres

HORS D'OEUVRES

Hors d'oeuvres admit multiple combinations and it would be impossible here to make a list of all of them. If in some occasion one of the ingredients is not avaliable, and it is not fundamental, this can be substituted by another equivalent.

Soup should be served only after the hors d'oeuvres if these are cold meats, preserves, etc. which do not require a previous preparation.

APERITIVES

Aperitives acquire category and appearance if they are presented harmonized with color combination and form and on a large silver tray with handles.

The cold aperitives should be served separate from the warm aperitives. The small aperitives show greater delicacy. Drinks to be served with aperitives could consist of vermouths, cocktails, whisky, sherry, gin, and fruit juices. Natural fruit juices are served cold and with sugar if desired.

ASPARAGUS

Asparagus are generally served with mayonnaise. Asparagus could also be served on top of sliced potatoes with a sauce.

BATTER FRIED SQUID

Servings: 6

6 squid (small or medium).—2 eggs.—1 cup olive oil.—1/2 cup of flour.—Salt to taste.

Clean squid, remove the tentacles, dry squid thoroughly. Cut body of squid in strips or rings without opening the body and in horizontal cuts. Dip squid in beaten eggs (containing salt) and then in flour. Fry in very hot oil. When squid is evenly brown (no more than 5 minutes) it is ready for serving.

CANAPÉS

Breads: these can be of various types and shapes e.g. molded bread, toasted, fried, geometrically shaped, slices, etc.—They are smeared with butter and topped with chorizo, hard boiled eggs, pickles, cheese, ensaladilla, ham, sardines, caviar, shrimp, crab tails, foie-gras, etc.

As you can see there are many variations possible for canapés. They only consist of a piece of bread, smeared with butter and then topped with whatever you wish.

Another possibility is to cover the bread with a spread of mayonnaise, crossed with strips of pimientos or anchovies.

Toasted bread spread with concentrated tomato sauce (ketchup) and topped with mashed hard boild egg yolk and chopped egg whites, is also very tasty. Sweet variations are also possible by using honey, powdered or shredded chocolate, etc.

CANNED FISH

All preserved fish can be served separately as hors d'oeuvres or on trays accompanied by salads. These preserves wether in oil or vinegar can be served along with pickles, cauliflower, radishes, carrots, hard boild eggs, etc.

GRIGS

1/2 lb. grigs.—2 tbls. oil.—2 cloves garlic (chopped).—Salt to taste.

The best grigs are the big and white ones, not the thin and dark.

Place well cleaned grigs in boiling water seasoned with salt, leaving them to boil for one minute. Drain the water from the grigs and dry them thoroughly with a cloth.

Place oil and garlic in casserole and allow to fry briefly. Add grigs and warm only as it is not necessary for them to fry.

The prepared grigs are served immediately in the same casserole or in small individuals.

GRIGS «AL AJILLO»

Place grigs in individual casseroles. Add boiling oil, chopped garlic and Guinea pepper. Stir quickly for several seconds and serve immediately in the same casseroles.

GRILLED SHRIMPS

1/2 lb. shrimps per person.—Salt.—Lemon juice.—Oil.

Wash shrimps but do not remove shells. Sprinkle with salt, lemon juice and oil. Place shrimps on a hot grill, sprinkling occasionally with water that contains a tablespoon of lemon juice and salt. The cooking time is about four minutes on one side and three on the other. The shrimps are done when their shells are orange red in color. Serve immediately.

HAM ROLLS

Sliced ham.—Butter.—Tunafish.—Sausages or veal.

The sausages are simmered in the frying pan. On top of ham spread with butter place either tunafish or the meat. Roll the ham and pinch with a toothpick.

It is also possible to mix the tunafish or the chopped meat with the butter to form a paste or cream with which you fill the ham.

Garnish with black olives, pickles, hard boiled eggs, etc.

«MEDIAS NOCHES»

Medias noches are buns of bread (sweet) that are filled with foie-gras cheese, butter and ham, sausages, etc.

MUSSELS

Mussels.—Flour.—Onion.—Powder of red pepper (paprika).—Garlic.—Salt.—Oil.

The mussels are cooked briefly in salted water, adding enough water to cover mussels. When cooked, place mussels on a tray or small plates and remove the shell to which the mussel in not attached.

Simmer in oil a small amount of onion and chopped garlic, adding afterwards a small amount of flour and paprika, which could be a little hot. After stirring briefly add some of the water in which the mussels were cooked. This water should be passed through a fine sieve to eliminate any residue from the mussels. The amount of water to add depends on the amount of sauce desired.

When the sauce has been cooked, put it through the blender to eliminate any lumps that may be present.

Pour boiling sauce over mussels and serve immediately.

OLIVES

There are several kinds of olives varying in size and in colour. Olives are also seasoned in various ways and some are stuffed with anchovies or pimiento. Olives can be served in many ways. If they are black serve them with chopped onion, paprika, oil and a bit of lemon juice, these ingredients being raw and placed on top of the olives.

If they are green serve them with pickles or use them to garnish other dishes.

POTATO BALLS

Mashed potatoes.—Grated cheese.

When the mashed potatoes are done, stir in grated cheese (the amount depending on individual taste). With a spoon form paste into balls, then roll in flour and fry. They can be served on a tray with pimientos olives, pickles, etc.

SANDWICHES

Bread (Rye, whole wheat, cracked wheat, buns, molded, etc.).

The bread is parted and between the two slices filled with a variation of things. The fill could consist of a combination of the following: ham, a variety of cold meats, cheese, eggs, tomatoes (whole or in a paste) mayonnaise, salads, fowl, sausages, pickles, tunafish, mushrooms, etc.

SHRIMPS «A LA GABARDINA»

Shrimps cooked in water and salt and then shelled.— The batter is similar to the one used for Soft Brains (see recipe under Fries, Pastes and Various Dishes).— Oil.

Dip the shelled shrimp in the batter and fry them in abundant hot oil. Variations of batter can be used. Serve them hot.

SHRIMPS IN GARLIC SAUCE

Peeled shrimps (approx. one dozen per person).— 2 cloves of garlic finely chopped.—A small piece of dry chilli pepper (Guinea pepper).—Oil or butter.— A pinch of salt.

Place the shrimps in individual casseroles. The shrimps are then sprinkled with the garlic and pieces of chili pepper. Add hot oil or butter, then salt to taste. Cook briefly and serve sizzling hot.

Salads

BEET SALAD

Beets.—Salt.—Garlic.—Parsley, if desired.—Oil.—Lemon.

Wash and clean beets, then boil in salty water with their skin. When beets are tender remove from heat and let them cool. Peel them and cut them into pieces. Sprinkle beets with fine salt, chopped garlic and parsley if desired. Add raw oil and a bit of lemon juice as you would do with many other salads. Stir all ingredients well so that flavor may be absorbed throughout, and serve it cold.

As most salads, this one is very nutritious.

Along with the beets, some carrots could be cooked, as a variation of this salad.

COOKED MIXED SALAD

Servings: 6

1 lb. boiled potatoes.—2 carrots cooked with the skin. 2 hard boiled eggs.—1 tbls. grated onion.—1 tbls.

15

vinegar.—1 pimiento.—1 tsp. salt.—1 cup of mayonnaise.—1 cup of olives (black or green, with pits removed).—1 cup of cooked peas.—Chopped pickles if desired.

Dice all vegetables and add to mayonnaise. Chop egg whites and mash yolks with the vinegar and salt. Blend all ingredients from both mixtures together. The salad may be garnished with excess pimiento cut in strips and the olives.

Tunafish can also be added, to variate.

POLISH SALAD

Servings: 6

1 lb. of potatoes previously cooked.—1/2 lb. of beets previously cooked.—1 hard boiled egg.—A little mustard if desired.—Spices if desired.—2 tbls. lemon juice.—Oil.—Salt.—Canned or fried sardines.—Olives 1 Whipped egg white.

With the hard boiled egg, the spices and salt well mashed, add a good squirt of oil slowly, making a creamy sauce to which the whipped egg white is added. Add lemon juice and taste salad for salt.

One pound of potatoes and half a pound of beets are cooked in water without salt until tender, drained, and cut into cubes.

Salt is then added, the potatoes and beets are covered with the previously prepared sauce and the tray can then be garnished with herrings or sardines and olives.

SUNDAY SALAD

Lettuce.—Olives black and green.—Tomatoes of the best type, without seeds.—Hard boiled eggs cut into slices.—Salad onions cut into slices.—A little parsley finely chopped.—Small radishes cleaned and cut into slices.—Finely chopped garlic.—Small peas fried

slightly.—One small can of tunafish broken into pieces (natural fried tunafish may be used instead). Lemon.—Finely grated salt.—Oil.

The amounts of the ingredients needed is up to the individual as people's taste vary. The important thing is to make a salad appetizing in appearance and taste.

Sprinkle vegetable ingredients with a mixture of oil and lemon, chopped garlic and salt. The lemon is substituting vinegar which is not good for ones health.

This salad could also contain other ingredients such as red pimientos, sliced carrots, etc.

The salad can be served on individual plates or in a large salad bowl.

TOMATO SALAD

Tomatoes of the best type.—Hard boiled eggs.— Mayonnaise.—Lettuce.—Onion.—Lemon.—Oil.— Salt.—Chopped garlic if desired.

The tomatoes are cut into slices and sprinkled with salt. The tomatoes are then sprinkled with three parts of oil and one part of lemon well blended. More lemon may be added. This is why quite often we do not specify amounts as we leave it up to the cook depending on his taste, and what ingredients he has available.

For this reason, some products can be substituted by others and the amount does not neccessarily have to be exact.

The hard boiled eggs are cut in halves and the yolks removed. The yolks are then mixed with the mayonnaise and put back in the egg white shell. When the eggs are filled they are placed inverted on the tomato slices. The lettuce and the chopped onion are sprinkled with lemon juice, oil, salt and chopped garlic if desired. This is then placed on the serving tray to fill in the spaces between the sliced tomatoes.

17

TUNA SALAD

**Potatoes are cooked in boiling water without salt.—
Canned tunafish or natural fried and cold.—Lettuce.—
Tomatoes.—Anchovies.—Olives, green or black,
preferably pitted.—Onion.—A little garlic and parsley.
Hard boiled egg.—Spices if desired.—Lemon.—Oil.—
Salt.**

When cooked, the potatoes are cubed and sprinkled
with a mixture made of two tbls. of lemon juice, three
tbls. of oil, salt to taste, and the spices if desired, all well
blended. Part of the mixture is saved for later use.

Adorn the potatoes with sliced tomatoes, lettuce,
tunafish, chopped onion olives, chopped garlic, hard boiled
egg, etc., and sprinkle with the remaining mixture.

To serve, the potatoes can be placed on the tray as a
base. The tunafish in the center, with the lettuce on the ends
and filling the ramaining spaces with eggs, olives, and
anchovies. The onion and the chopped garlic along with
the parsley can be sprinkled on top or mixed with the potatoes priviously.

The tomatoes can form flowers with the lettuce or used
as the base for the eggs.

VEGETABLE SALAD

**Hearts of artichokes, peas, carrots, asparagus,
potatoes, etc.—The total weight of these vegetables
should be approximately two pounds.—Lemon juice.—
White pepper.—Mustard.—Chili pepper if desired.—
Oil and salt.**

Reserve the asparagus to adorn serving tray. The rest
of the vegetables are cooked in boiling water without salt.
After cooking the vegetables are drained and then parted
into equal pieces.

The cooked vegetables are covered with a mixture of
lemon juice, a good squirt of oil, the spices if desired and

salt to taste. Stir ingredients lightly so flavor can be absorbed throughout.

The salad is adorned with asparagus that have also been seasoned with the mixture.

Seafood

CLAMS

The same as oysters, the clams decompose rapidly
after they are dead. For this reason, they are cooked when
they are still alive and in the similar way as the oysters.
They can also be eaten raw with strawberries or lemon.

CLAMS «A LA MARINERA»

**Two pounds of clams.—One tbls. of butter.—Oil.—
Onion.—Garlic.—Parsley.—Two tbls. of flour.—
One cup of white wine.**

Wash clams well and cook them in the white wine.
Add enough water so clams are covered. As clams are
cooking, skim off the foam that forms. At the same time,
stir the clams so that all sand is released. When they are
open, remove them from liquid with skimmer and allow
water to settle.

While the clams are cooking, prepare the sauce which

consists of one tbls. of butter, two tbls. of oil, three or four tbls. of chopped onion, one clove of garlic, and a bit of parsley also well chopped.

When all these ingresients have been fried briefly, add the two tbls. of flour and continue to fry momentarily.

The clams are now added to the sauce and also the water in which they were cooked, being careful not to stir up the water. If preferred, the water may be passed through a very fine sieve in order to eliminate the sand. Serve hot.

LOBSTER

The best lobster is the female lobster when she is in heat, and the male lobster the rest of the time.

The lobster season is in spring and at the end of the summer.

The lobster should be cooked with the legs and tail tied to prevent it from breaking and loosing blood when agitated.

BOILED LOBSTER WITH SAUCE

Lobster, approximatély one and a half pounds.—Salt, one tbls. per quart of water.—One cup of mayonnaise. 1/4 cup of lemon juice.—1 tbls. of sugar.

In a large pot having a tight fitting cover, bring salted water rapidly to boiling. Grasp lobster by the back and plunge the head first into the water. There should be enough water to cover the lobster. The water is again brought to a boiling point, the pot is covered and alowed to simmer fifteen to twenty minutes. Drain hot water from lobster and then cover with cold water to chill. Drain again and place lobster shell-side down on a cutting board.

Twist off the tail, the two large claws and the smaller ones. Slit the bony membrane on the underside of the tail. The intestinal vein is then removed and discarded. Cut tail through crosswise into pieces (one to two inches) Cut the body of the lobster through completely lengthwise and through shell. Remove and discard the intestinal vein running lengthwise through the center of the body. Remove and discard stomach (a small sac which lies in the head), the lungs (which lie in the upper body cavity, between meat and shell).

The green liver and coral (red roe) can be used to garnish. Cut the body into one to two inch pieces.

The pieces of lobster are chilled and when ready to serve, all the pieces are placed on a tray with the shell-side up to resemble a whole lobster.

The sauce is prepared by blending together one cup of mayonnaise, a quarter cup of lemon juice and one tbls. of sugar. The sauce is chilled and poored over lobster when ready to serve.

OYSTERS

Oysters have a similar chemical composition as milk. They are very nutritious and can be considered as a complete aliment of easy assimilation. They are an excellent aperitive as they arouse the appetite. Rich in protein, 18 oysters supplement the necessary protein for one adult in 24 hours. They are recommendable as reconstituent since they contain iron and copper necessary for the hemoglobin in the blood. They also contain iodine, calcium, phosphorus, manganese, zinc, and they are rich in vitamins A, B, C, and D.

They are more nutritious than raw liver. People on a salt restricted diet should not eat oysters.

Oysters should be eaten alive and raw (as they decompose easily when dead) with a squirt of lemon, placing them previously on a hot plate in order to open them.

The oysters which open by themselves or are open when you buy them, should be descarded as they are in a period of dehydration. This happens during hot weather, and this measure should be taken as a precaution.

The oysters which are well closed are the best and the freshest, but in the months of May, June, July, and August one should take extra care when buying seaford, due to the heat.

Oysters can transmit intestinal and typhoid infections

if they come from a contaminated hatchery. Because of this, it is recommended to squeeze a lemon over the oysters before eating them as the acidity of the juice destroys most of the germs.

The lemon juice is more effective than that of strawberries

ROASTED «VIEIRAS O CONCHAS DE PEREGRINO»

With 6 vieiras you need 3 tbls. of chopped onion.— A small clove of chopped garlic.—A branch of parsley. A small amount of pepper and clove if you desire.— One beaten egg.—One tbls. of bread crumbs.—One tbls. of oil or two of butter.

Remove the animals from their shell, chop them into small pieces and then mix them with the other ingredients to form a paste.

Fill the shells again with the paste and place them in the oven on a refractory plate containing a little water.

It is possible to add more of the ingredient you like best and you can also add cognac, champagne, etc.

SEAFOOD CASSEROLE

One pound of mussels.—Half a pound of shrimp or sea crabs.—Half a pound of prawns.—Half a pound of clams.—Half a pound of small squids.—Two tbls. of butter and four tbls. of oil.—One large onion.— Two cloves of garlic.—One branch of parsley.—Two regular tomatoes without their skin.—One cup of dry sherry.—Small leaf of laurel.

Clams and mussels are opened by cooking them for several minutes in boiling water. The water is drained and the shellfish rinsed well to remove the sand and all particles they may contain.

Brown the onion lightly in the oil and butter and add the two cloves of garlic whole. Separate onion to a plate and remove the garlic which you mash with the parsley.

When these two ingredients are mashed, mix them with the onion and place them on a plate. The clean squids are cut into pieces and fried lightly. When this is done, add the mixture of garlic, onion and parsley. Remove seeds from tomatoes, peel them, cut them into pieces and add them to the squids.

The other seafoods that are not cooked, are washed and cleaned and added as well. When these ingredients have fried slightly add the water from the clams being careful that none of the sediment gets into the frying pan. Leave everything to cook until the sauce is a little thick.

The casserole is now ready to be served.

SEAFOODS

In Spain seafood is very popular. It is of excellent quality and many types of seafood are sold at quite low prices. Foreigners too, love the variety of seafood available and there are many types with which they are not familiar. Some of the popular seafoods in Spain are: mussels, shrimps, prawns, clams, squid, oysters, lobster, crabs, sea spiders, and barnicles. Some shell fish such as the oysters and clams are very good when eaten raw with only a few drops of lemon juice or a special sauce. A good white wine is a fine accompaniment for most seafood.

SEA URCHINS

The best sea urchins are the green and black ones. They are open at the flat side or the base. Remove the mouth and with the scissors cut off the flat part. The water which they have inside is discarded and they are then cooked in salted water or they are eaten raw with lemon. The cooking time is very brief.

It is possible to cook sea urchins whole and after cooking, use the water they contain to make a sauce.

Sea urchins contain a great quantity of iodine.

Various types of cold meats

FIRST CLASS «CHORIZO»

**Three parts of pork meat for every one part of «tocino».
Ten pounds of pork meat from the shoulder blade.
This can be substituded by eight pounds of regular
pork meat and three pounds of «tocino».—One clove
of garlic for every two pounds of meat.—Half a pound
of paprika.—Nine yards of pork intestines.—Half a
pound of coarse salt.**

Once the meat and «tocino» have been cleaned of
skin, nerves, and bones, cut it into pieces and put it through
the meat grinder. The peeled cloves of garlic are mashed
in a mortar. To the meat add the garlic, salt, and paprika.
Mix everything thoroughly and let it stand from 8 to 10
hours in a cool place covered with a fine cloth (cheese
cloth).

When this time has passed taste the meat mixture to
see if it is satisfactorily spiced remembering that the final
flavor has not been completely absorbed. At this point
you can rectify the taste. Once again let mixture stand
for sixteen hours this time.

25

After the curing period, start to stuff the well cleaned intestines with the mixture. If the intestines are dry, they should be wetted previously. Tie the intestines with string well spaced in order to make individual «chorizos» (take into consideration that they will shrink when drying). If you are using fresh intestines, wash them well in vinegar and salt, turning them inside out and rinse them well in cold water. «Chorizos» are dried by hanging them up in a cold open place. «Chorizos» may also be smoked if desired.

«MORCILLAS» FROM ASTURIAS

Since each region has a different way to make «morcilla» we will describe here the typical one for the Asturian «fabada».

One quart of pork blood.—Four pounds of onion.— Half a pound of pumpkin.—One and one third pounds of pork lard.—Paprika and salt.—Pieces of unsmoked bacon.—Wild marjoram if desired.

Chop the four pounds of onion and form it into a flat surface in a big container. Place the chopped lard and bacon on top of the onion. Season these ingredients with salt, paprika and add the pumpkin finely minced. If desired you may add a bit of wild marjoram.

On top of all this pour the blood of the pork.

When the fresh blood is collected from the pig it is necessary to stir it immediately with your hands or with a wooden spoon in order to prevent the blood from coagulating.

Stir all ingredients well and let stand for one hour. Taste it and correct the seasoning if it is not satisfactory.

The mixture is stuffed into the intestines of pork or cow and tied with string every twelve inches.

Place the tied «morcillas» for two minutes in a large container holding boiling water. Drain the water from the «morcillas» and place them to dry on a cloth. The «morcillas» are hung up to dry (similar to «chorizos») but they are not completely dry until they are black in colour.

«Morcillas» can be conserved all year around.

If smoking «morcillas» you should not use aromatic woods like pine, as they give a bad taste.

PORK «FOIE-GRAS»

Half a pound of pork liver.—Two thirds of a pound of pork lard.—Salt and a small amount of pepper if desired.—A small truffle very well chopped if desired.

Reserve a piece of the lard for later use. Remove the skin and the nerves from the liver and chop it very finely. Mix in the lard (not the reserved) salt and spices if desired. Spices should be eliminated when the «foie-gras» is to be eaten by children.

With the ingredients well mixed, make a roll and cover it with the reserved piece of lard. Place roll in a double boiler, allowing it to curdle.

The cooking time will be fifteen minutes if the double boiler is placed in the oven with strong heat.

SAUSAGES

One part of loin, another of meat and another of fresh fat.—Salt, garlic, and not too many spices.— Lamb intestines.

Chop the loin meat and fat, and season with salt and spices being careful not to put too much. If you desire red sausages, substitute the spices by sweet paprika as it is only the white sausages that contain spices. After 4 or 5 hours, stuff the lamb intestines with the mixture (as in former recipes) and tie in smaller pieces than for the «chorizos».

Bouillons, soups and «potajes»

ASTURIAN «FABADA»

Servings: 6

Five cups of white broad beans which have been soaked overnight.—One half pound of ham.—One half pound of sausage («chorizo»).—One half pound of blood sausage (Asturian).—One half pound salted pork (spine with bones).—One can of red pimientos.— One half tsp. pepper.—One half tsp. saffron.—Salt to taste.

Today there are many variations of «fabada» which originally was a dish consisting of a lamb and bean stew. Since there are variations, you too can subtract or add whatever you want, making sure that your ingredients are in good taste and compatible. On a cold day, a serving of hot «fabada» is very satisfying. It can be served with a fresh salad and a light dessert. To the previously soaked beans add ten cups of cold water and place on stove to boil. Once the water is boiling add the ham, salted pork, «chorizo», blood sausage, the saffron and the pepper, and cook until the beans are tender. When cooked taste the dish for salt, and about ten minutes before serving add the pimientos which should be sliced finely.

CHICKPEA «DE VIGILIA»

Servings: 4

Two cups of chickpeas which have been soaked overnight.—One clove of garlic, peeled.—One half tsp. salt.—One tsp. baking soda.—One medium onion, sliced.

Before soaking the chickpeas, they should be sorted in order to eliminate any that may contain bits of shell or stones. To chickpeas add the salt, baking soda, whole garlic, chopped onion and add warm water so that the level is about two inches above the chickpeas. Cook the ingredients uncovered until the chickpeas are just tender. They should be boiling gently and covered with water all the time. If more water needs to be added, use boiling water. The cooking time will be three hours more or less, depending on the peas. When the chickpeas are cooked remove the garlic and the onion.

CASTILIAN «COCIDO»

One handful of chickpeas per person.—A piece of salted ham.—A piece of «chorizo».—A piece of third class beef, a piece of fat and a bone.—Half an onion and leeks.—Fine spaghetti for the soup.— Cabbage, lettuce and tomatoes for the salad.—Salt, oil and lemon.

Soak chickpeas overnight in warm water. To cook, place chickpeas in boiling water in a normal pot or in a pressure cooker, along with the oil and meats. Allow this to cook until peas are tender (three to four hours if using an ordinary pot, but if using a pressure cooker, cook them for only half an hour). When they are cooked add the salt and leave them for a few minutes.

Place the cabbage, leeks, onion and garlic to cook in a separate pot. When these are cooked, drain them and add salt along with a little bit of paprika fried in hot oil.

The water from the chickpeas is used for making the soup to which you can add the fine spaghetti or whatever you may desire.

Make the fresh salad.

The soup is served first. Second, serve the chickpeas on a tray along with the cabbage and leeks. The meat may be served separately or on the same tray. The salad is eaten along with the second course.

CATALONIAN «ESCUDELLA»

One half cup of white beans.—One half cup of chickpeas.—A piece of «tocino» and a blood sausage. Three or four regular potatoes.—One cup of chopped cabbage.—One half cup of rice.—One cup of spaghetti broken.—Salt, onion, garlic, parsley and other herbs if desired.

Leave beans and chickpeas to soak overnight. For cooking, place them in boiling water with the «tocino». After cooking for one hour add the cabbage and the blood sausage which is tied at the ends, two cloves of garlic not peeled, a piece of onion and the herbs.

Half an hour before everything is completely cooked you add the rice and the spaghetti seasoning with salt. Serve everything together on a tray.

CLAM SOUP

Servings: 4

One pound of clams, medium size.—One leaf of laurel.—A branch of parsley.—One small onion.—

One clove of garlic.—Oil.—Salt.—White wine.— One half pound of rice.

Wash the clams and cook them in water with a good squirt of white wine and salt to season. Once they are cooked and open, place them in another casserole. The water in which they were cooked is let to stand to add more water and cook the rice with it. The proportion should be three parts of water per one of rice.

Boil the water. Chop finely the onion, parsley and garlic and fry them lightly in oil. To the boiling water add the oil and the last three ingredients. Then add the rice stirring it for a few minutes to prevent it from sticking on the bottom. Boil for 10 minutes. Take it away from the fire but keep it covered so it continues boiling slowly. After another 10 minutes add the clams without shell and serve.

CONSOMMÉ

Servings: 6

One half pound of chicken.—One bone of beef.— One half pound of beef (third class meat).—One half of a small onion.—Two or three cloves of garlic unpeeled.—One cup of white wine.—A small piece of salted ham.—Salt.—One branch of parsley.—Two regular tomatoes.—One egg white.

Add all the ingredients except salt to two quarts of cold water and cook for 4 hours. Maintain the casserole well covered and skim frequently.

Once it is cooked pass it through a wet cloth. To clarify it, add the beaten egg white mixed with 2 tbls. of the liquid and the tomatoes. Mix everything boil for two minutes and filter again through the wet cloth.

This soup known as «consomé» can be served hot or cold. Pieces of fried bread can be added if desired. Serve in cups with handles.

FISH BOUILLON

**One half a pound of fish scraps.—Two small carrots.—
Two small onions.—One leek.—One clove of garlic.
One branch of parsley.—Two regular tomatoes.**

Cook in cold water the fish scraps and the rest of the
ingredients all well chopped. Cook for half an hour. If
you are using a pressure cooker cook only for 8 minutes.
Drain and reserve the liquid.

Some shell fish like crabs, shrimps, clams, etc. can be
added to the liquid. First they must be boiled without
peeling them. After they are boiled, peel them, and remove
shells. Now they can be added to the reserved liquid. At
this point you can also add small pieces of fried fish. The
dish is now ready to be served.

FISH SOUP «BOUILLABAISE»

It is considered the queen of the soups. All kinds of
white fish can be used. The best are:

**Mackerel, sea bass, eels, grouper, etc.—Choose three
of them or half a pound of each.—One lobster.—Three
prawns.—One half pound of clams.—One pound
of mussels.—Three medium carrots, chopped.—Two
tbls. of onion, chopped.—One leek.—One half a
pound of tomatoes without seeds.—A few branches
of parsley.—One clove of garlic.—A small leaf of
laurel.—A pinch of saffron.—Oil.—Salt.—Molded
bread.**

The fish is cut into thick slices. The mussels and clams
are washed and cooked in boiling water, stirring in order
to release all the sand they may contain. Let sediment and
use the water for the soup. The prawns, mussels, and clams
are put in the water again.

The onion, carrots, tomatoes and the rest of the
ingredients are fried lightly, then add the lobster meat
cut into slices, and also the rest of the fish. Stir briefly.

32

Put all these ingredients, and also the prawns, mussels, clams and water in a big casserole and add more water if necessary to cover all of them.

Add salt to season and let it boil hard in the beginning, then softly for 10 minutes. You can boil it some extra minutes if necessary.

The bread toasted in slices is smeared with garlic and covered with butter and then fried or toasted again.

The soup can be served alone or with the shellfish. Bread should be served in a small basket or on a different-plate.

FOWL GIBLETS SOUP

A few bones.—One small piece of ham.—Garlic.— Parsley.—Leek.—Fowl giblets.—Hard boiled eggs or pieces of fried bread if desired.

Put enough water in a casserole considering that it will have to boil for three hours. Boil the ingredients to make the soup. You can also put the giblets in if you wish. Once it is cooked, separate the giblets, and drain the other ingredients to use the liquid. The liver is mashed and mixed with the liquid. Remove the bones from the giblets and chop them finely before adding them to the soup. Add salt to season.

Hard boiled egg, cubes of fried bread, a bit of flour fried in butter, etc. could be added to the soup if desired. Serve hot.

GALICIAN BOUILLON

A piece of pork (from the shoulder).—A few salted ribs.—A piece of «tocino».—A cup of kidney beans soaked over night.—Half a dozen of regular size potatoes.—A small cabbage.—A small piece of aged pork lard.—A «chorizo» or paprika to give colour.

Cook all the ingredients except the lard and paprika in two quarts of cold water. When everything is tender, melt the lard and paprika in a frying pan and add to other ingredients. Add salt a few minutes before serving.

GALICIAN POT

Servings: 6

> **Two pounds of cabbage.—One pound of white beans.— Two ounces of pork lard.—One and a half pounds of beef.—A piece of salted ham.—A piece of blood sausage.—One pork sausage.**

The beans are soaked overnight.

Place all the ingredients except the pork lard into the pressure cooker. When everything is cooked add the salt. With the liquid make a soup. You can add to the soup fine and small slices of bread, some potatoes and a small amount of cabbage and beans. The pork lard is melted and added to the soup. Serve the meat and vegetables on two separate trays.

GARLIC SOUP

> **Bread.—Pork lard.—Garlic.—Salt.—Paprika.**

Boil water. Cut paper thin slices of bread. Melt the pork lard in the frying pan. Mash one or two cloves of garlic in the mortar, depending on the amount of soup. Add also the salt and paprika. When the pork lard is boiling, pour it into the mortar and mix it with the ingredients present. Add the mix to the boiling water. Add the bread slices to the water. Take the pot away from the fire. Serve after 10 minutes.

«GAZPACHO»

Servings: 4

> **Six regular tomatoes.—Two small onions.—Three regular cucumbers.—Two glasses of water.—Salt.—**

Paprika if desired.—A few slices of bread.—A piece of ice if desired.—Garlic.—Parsley.—Lemon.

Wash, clean and slice the tomatoes, onions and cucumbers. Add the garlic finely chopped to these ingredients Mix a good squirt of lemon with two squirts of oil and the salt. Stir everything together. Chop the ice to serve. One variation of the «Gazpacho» is to pass all the ingredients through a blender.

HEN BOUILLON

One half pound of hen.—One handful of chickpeas.— A good beef bone.—A branch of parsley.—One clove of garlic.—One half of a small onion.—Two small carrots.—Salt.—A piece of salted ham.

Clean the hen and burn the small feathers that may be present. Place the hen and the rest of the ingredients in approximately two quarts of water. Leave the salt to be added when everything is cooked.

The cooking time goes from three to four hours. If you are using a pressure cooker, the time would be around half an hour. In this case instead of two quarts, put only one and a half.

Once it is cooked, drain it, add the salt and serve it.

Colour can be given to the soup by adding a pinch of saffron in the beginning.

HERB SOUP OR «SOPA JULIANA»

Servings: 4

A small carrot.—A small turnip.—One regular potato. One dozen of string beans.—A few leaves of cabbage.— A few leaves of spinach.—One cauliflower heart.— Two or three asparagus.—Two leeks.—A few beef bones.—A piece of salted ham.—Oil.—Salt.—Paprika if desired.

All kinds of fresh vegetables can be used. All vegetables are cleaned and peeled then cut into strips. Cook the vegetables together with the bones in boiling water. Vegetables should be slightly covered with water but not too much as vegetables do not absorb very much water while cooking.

Allow vegetables to cook until they are tender, add the salt and leave for a few minutes. Remove the bones making sure that there are no small pieces left in the soup. The soup is served hot after seasoning with oil or grease.

MASHED POTATOES

In Spain this dish is more fluid than the regular stiff mashed potatoes, it is more like a thick soup.

Servings: 4

Six good size potatoes.—Onion.—Garlic.— Palsley. A little white wine.—Pimientos if desired.—Carrots Beets if desired.—Oil or butter.—A beef bone.—A little beef meat if you like.

The potatoes, peeled, cleaned, and parted are placed to cook together with the other ingredients also cleaned and parted. The salt is added when everything is cooked. Remove the bone and pass everything, except the meat, through a fine grinder or blender. To serve, the meat may be chopped and added to the dish.

MEAT BOUILLON

Carrots.—Leeks.—Half a pound of beef or veal.— Five pounds of bones.—Garlic.—Parsley.—Salt.— Onion.

Cook together one leek, one regular onion, a few branches of parsley, one clove of garlic, clean but not peeled, the bones and the meat, covered in water.

Cook ingredients until there is only one cup of liquid

remaining. Let, it cool and remove the fat. Season the soup with salt and store it in a cool place.

To use, you add one tbls. of the soup to half a quart of hot or boiling water, and the soup is then ready to serve. If you want it more concentrated, reduce the amount of water.

MENESTRA

Servings: 6

One half pound of veal (cartilage, meat from the breast).—One half pound of chicken.—A good bone.— One fifth of a pound of salted ham.—A piece of «tocino».—Salt.—Garlic.—Parsley.—One leaf of laurel.—One half a pound of potatoes, new if possible. Four artichokes.—Two regular carrots.—Lettuce or other tender vegetable.—One half a pound of broad beans.—One half a pound of peas.—Some tips of natural asparagus. If canned asparagus are used, they are added at the end.—Two small salad onions.— One leek.

Everything is cooked together in boiling water. The garlic is whole but the vegetables parted. The meat also is parted and fried slightly in a frying pan before adding it to the vegetables. Remove the outer leaves of the artichokes and also the hard tip, using only the heart of the artichoke.

When everything is cooked, remove the garlic and the bone. To serve you can add small pieces of fried bread if you wish.

POTATOES

The new potatoes have better taste and are more pleasant and healthy than the old ones.

Potatoes can be prepared in a thousand ways, alone, with meats, with vegetables, etc.

Potatoes should not be washed after cutting them,

because in contact with the water, they lose the starch and some of its vitamins. They should be washed after peeling them but before cutting them.

POTATOES «A LA IMPORTANCIA»

Servings: 4

Two pounds of potatoes.—One quarter of a pound of ground meat.—A bit of salted ham if desired.—Garlic. Parsley.—Flour.—One egg.—Oil.—White wine.

Peel and wash the potatoes and cut them into slices of less than half an inch in thickness. Sprinkle salt on top, dip them in flour and after in a well beaten egg. Fry the potatoes in hot oil and then place them in a pot containing white wine and a little water. The wine and the water should be hot.

In the same oil as you fried the potatoes, you also fry the meat, ham and a few pieces of bread. In a mortar mash the fried bread, the garlic, parsley and add a little bit of water. This is poured over the potatoes as well as the meat without the oil. Taste for salt and let everything cook, again until the potatoes are tender. If you want to make this dish more economical you can eliminate the meat, the ham and the egg.

POTATOE SOUFFLÉ

Potatoes.—Oil.—Salt.

Wash and peel potatoes. Cut them into rather thick slices and fry them in a good amount of hot oil, frying a few at a time so that they will not stick to each other. Remove them with a skimmer and let them cool a little. Keeping the oil hot, start to fry the potatoes once again and they should puff up.

38

PUFFS FOR THE SOUP

With the paste from the recipe for «Wind Puffs» form small balls, as they will expand a lot. They are fried in hot oil.

They are added to the soup or bouillon at the time of serving.

These can be substituded by cubes of fried bread.

RICE SOUP

Servings: 6

One good beef bone.—Giblets of chicken.—One half pound of rice.—One tbls. of butter.—One regular carrot.—One leek.—One clove of garlic.—One branch of parsley.—A small truffle.—A hard boiled egg.— Onion.

In two quarts of fresh water cook the bone, giblets, onion, parsley, carrot, and the garlic which should be cleaned but not peeled. If using the pressure cooker put only one quart and a half, of water.

When everything is cooked, it is drained and the giblets are chopped and added to the liquid. If desired you can also chop and add the egg and truffle. Season this with salt and add the rice to cook. This dish is not served too hot. To this dish you can also add small pieces of white fish, pieces of ham etc.

SEAFOOD SOUP

Clams.—Shrimps.—Crabs.—Mussels.—Barnicles.— Onion.—Garlic.—Parsley.—Tomato.—Laurel.— Oil.—Salt.—Pepper.—Macaroni.—Grated cheese.

Everything, except the macaroni and cheese, is placed to cook in water. Once it is cooked, put it in the mortar and grind it. Then put it through a wet cloth to avoid small pieces of shell from getting into the soup. In this liquid cook the macaroni, add a bit of grated cheese and taste for salt.

STEWED POTATOES

> **Two pounds of potatoes.—A quarter of a cup of white wine.—A piece of «tocino» or ham.—Onion.—Red pimientos.—Salt.—Parsley.—Oil.—Paprika.—You may add tomatoes if you like, but the acid from the tomatoes does not go well with the potatoes.**

Once the potatoes are peeled and parted, they can be lightly fried in oil if desired. The rest of the ingredients except the «tocino» are chopped and cooked together with the potatoes. The «tocino» is parted and mixed with oil. Add to the oil and «tocino» a bit of paprika. This should be poured on top of the potatoes and cooked vegetables. Taste for salt.

If meat is going to be added to the potatoes, it should be fried lightly before putting it to cook with the rest of the ingredients.

STUFFED POTATOES

> **Three pounds of regular potatoes with good shape.—One half pound of chopped meat.—Two eggs.—Garlic, parsley, onion.—Oil or butter.—Pimientos and tomatoes.—Flour.—One quarter of a cup of white wine.**

Once the potatoes are peeled and washed, hollow them out through only one hole at the end of the potato. A special apparatus to hollow potatoes is sold at the stores.

The onion, garlic, a branch of parsley and a few tomatoes without seeds and peeled, are chopped and mixed with the ground meat. Add salt and a beaten egg and mix everything thoroughly. With this mix, stuff the potatoes.

Dip them in flour and in the other beaten egg and fry

40

them in oil or butter. Then put them in boiling water to which we have added the wine, being careful so that they do not break. They are served in the same sauce.

VEGETABLE BOUILLON

One regular potato.—One big leaf of vegetable (cauliflower, cabbage, etc.)—One regular carrot.— One half of a small onion.—One leek or a clove of garlic.—One leaf of laurel.—A branch of parsley.— A piece of «tocino».—Paprika.—Two regular tomatoes.—A piece of red or green pimiento.—A piece of salted ham.—Some beef bones.—Oil.

Cook all the ingredients except the oil, in two quarts of boiling water. Cook for approximately half an hour. Once it is cooked, taste for salt.

To the oil or melted «tocino» add a pinch of paprika to give some colour, and add this mixture to the potato and rest of the vegetables. Put them in the grinder and add later on some pieces of hard boiled egg.

VEGETABLE «POTAJE»

One half a pound of white beans.—One half a pound of cabbage.—One half a pound of potatoes.—Two or three regular carrots.—Half a small onion.—Two cloves of garlic.—A small turnip.—A few radishes.— One «chorizo».—One blood sausage.—A piece of «tocino».—A beef bone.—One half pound of beef.

Soak the white beans overnight. Place all the ingredients to boil in warm water, in pieces. The garlic should be removed before serving. When they are cooked add the salt. The meats are served on another plate.

Vegetables

Vegetables are rich in vitamins and minerals. Vegetables should be fresh and with intense colour.

It is necessary to wash them well since they always carry dirt but do not leave them too long in water as they lose their nutritional value. Drain them well or dry them after washing.

All dry vegetables like chickpeas, lentils, beans, etc. should be soaked overnight in clean water. This operation makes the cooking much easier. To cook use the same water in which they were soaked since much of the nutritional value is passed to the water.

ARTICHOKES «A LA GRIEGA»

One dozen of artichokes.—One half glass of white wine.—One beef bone (knee bone).—A piece of ham.—Dwarf onions.—Garlic.—Parsley.—Oil. Salt.

Wash the artichokes, remove the hard outer leaves, cut off the tips and put them in the liquid that is prepared with the bones, ham, ten to twelve little onions, a clove of garlic, parsley, salt, half a glass of white wine, and let it cook.

When they are cooked, they are served without the liquid and garnished with the onions or with a special vegetable sauce. This could be: Vinegar sauce, sauce bechamel, etc. (Recipes to be found under Sauces and Garnishes). If you want to be more economical, they can be cooked in plain water and salt.

The liquid is drained from the other ingredients and it can then be used by itself as a bouillon or used to make a soup.

CARROTS «GLASEADAS»

One pound of carrots.—Two tbls. of butter.—Sugar.—Salt.

Scrape or peel the carrots, wash them and cut them into slices or strips. Cook them in boiling water. When they are almost cooked, add a bit of salt and they are allowed to cook a few minutes more. Drain the water and place the carrots in an earthenware pot. Now, pour boiling water to the carrots only until they are covered. Add the butter and one half tbls. of sugar. Boil for five minutes, cover them and place them into the oven at high heat until the water is reduced but without letting the carrots get dry. Serve them hot. They can be used to accompany meat.

CAULIFLOWER WITH CHEESE «AU GRATIN»

One cauliflower.—Onion.—Garlic.—Parsley.—Butter.—Salt.—Cheese.

Place pieces of onion, parsley and a few cloves of garlic in cold water. When the water is boiling add the cauliflower well washed and parted in big pieces. Season with salt. When tender, drain the water and place the cauliflower in an earthenware casserole, sprinkle it with grated cheese, balls of butter, and bake it at medium heat for a few minutes.

43

One cauliflower.—Oil.—Paprika.—Lemon.—Salt.— Garlic.

Cook cleaned cauliflower in salted water, previously cut into pieces. In hot oil, fry lightly a chopped clove of garlic. When slightly brown, remove the pan from the fire, add a little paprika and a squirt of lemon juice. All this is poured over the drained cauliflower, it is stirred lightly so that the flavor may be absorbed throughout the cauliflower, and serve hot on a tray.

You could also fry the cauliflower in the frying pan but since cauliflower is a tender vegetable, it is very likely to brake.

CAULIFLOWER «REBOZADA»

Cauliflower.—Oil.—Salt.—Egg.—Flour.—Milk.

Wash the cauliflower, brake it into pieces and place it to boil in salted water. Once the cauliflower is cooked, it is drained and dipped in a mixture of whipped egg and flour. (This mixture should not be too stiff) It is fried in abundant hot oil.

CAULIFLOWER «AU GRATIN»

One cauliflower.—Sauce «bechamel».—Onion.—Garlic.—Salt.—Grated cheese.—Bread crumbs may substitute the cheese if you want.—Parsley.

Place pieces of onion, a few cloves of garlic without peeling them, parsley and salt, in cold water. When the water is boiling add the cauliflower broken into big pieces and allow to cook. When it is tender, drain it and place it in an earthenware casserole which has been previously coated with oil or butter.

Sprinkle it with grated cheese or bread crumbs and pieces of butter. Place it in the oven for ten minutes under high heat until the butter is melted and the cheese or bread forms a crust.

CAULIFLOWER WITH SAUCE

Cook cauliflower similar to the recipe for Cauliflower with cheese «au gratin». Place it on a tray and cover it with sauce «bechamel», mayonnaise sauce, tomato sauce, etc.

FRIED EGGPLANTS

Eggplants.—Salt.—Sugar.—Oil.—Flour.—Egg.

Wash and cut eggplants into fine slices. Place them in salted water and leave them for half an hour to eliminate the bitterness. When this time is passed, drain the eggplants, dip them in flour, then in a whipped egg and fry them lightly in oil. If they are fried too much they will get hard. Sprinkle them with sugar or salt. Serve hot.

«LACON CON GRELOS»

«Grelos» are one of the three tipes of leaves of the turnip plant.
Servings: 5

One pound of «lacon» (this is cured ham).—Two pounds of potatoes.—One «chorizo» per person.— One half pound of «grelos».

Soak the «lacon» in water one day in advance. Next day place the «lacon» in cold water and cook it. While the water is still hot add the «grelos», the chopped potatoes and the «chorizos».

Taste for salt when everything is almost cooked and serve it hot.

MUSHROOMS «A LA CREMA»

One half pound of mushrooms.—Onion.—Garlic.— Parsley.—Butter.—Oil.—Flour.—Lemon.

If canned mushrooms are going to be used, drain the liquid from the can and chop the mushrooms. If the mushrooms are natural, wash them well since they contain a lot of earth. Chop them in pieces, not too small. Place them in a frying pan with onion, garlic, parsley (very well chopped) until the onion gets brown in colour. Then add the salt. Sprinkle with flour and with a squirt of lemon, stir them gently and place them on a serving tray.

NATURAL ARTICHOKES

Artichokes are rich in iron, iodine and mineral salts. Artichokes should be fresh and firm. To cook them you should always pull the outer leaves off and remove the tip since it is the hardest part. Cook them in boiling water with salt and a squirt of lemon.

NATURAL PEAS

The best peas are the green tender ones. The big ones with a light green colour and hard skin are not so good.

Peas.—Butter or oil.

Place peas in a casserole with a little oil or butter. Cover the casserole and heat them for a few minutes moving the casserole to stir them frequently. Then add a little amount of water and let them cook with the steam. Salt should be added at the same time as the water.

Peas serve as garnish for any dish of meats or vegetables. They can also be eaten after frying them in oil.

PEAS WITH HAM

Peas.—Salted ham with a little fat.—Butter or oil.— Onion.—Parsley.—A few hearts of lettuce.—Water.— Salt.—Garlic.—Fried bread.

Place the ham chopped in pieces in a frying pan with oil or butter. Add the peas with a lot of onion, the parsley in branches, the hearts of the lettuce and one whole clove of garlic. Add the salt, being careful since the ham is already salted. After cooking for a few minutes, add a little bit of water and allow to cook gently. When cooked, remove the parsley, onion, and garlic.

To the liquid add a little bit of flour to thicken it. You can also add crushed almonds or walnuts.

The peas and ham can be served with or without sauce on a tray garnished with cubes of fried bread.

«PISTO»

One half pound of potatoes.—A big tomato.—A small pimiento.—A big slice of salted ham with some fat on it.—A medium onion.—One clove of garlic.—Parsley.—Oil.—Salt.—Two eggs.

Peel the potatoes, wash them and cut them into pieces (cubes). Add the salt and place them to fry in a frying pan. A few moments later, add the ham chopped into cubes, the chopped onion, the garlic and the pimiento. Let it cook and then add the tomato. The tomato should be peeled, without seeds and chopped finely. Mix it with the rest of the ingredients. Add the two beaten eggs and season with salt. Stir gently until everything is thoroughly mixed. You can serve it when the eggs are done.

ROASTED PIMIENTOS

The pimientos should be thick with a lot of meat, pre-ferable red and sweet. Pimientos can be roasted in two different ways:

1.—Wash them and place them in the oven, turning them until the skin can be easily removed.

2.—They can be cut in two or more pieces longwise. Then remove the seads, coat them with oil and chopped garlic and place them in the oven.

Roasted pimientos are used to accompany meats, rice, eggs, etc. They can be eaten alone or seasoned with salt and lemon.

To remove the skin from the roasted pimientos, wrap them immediately in a cloth. After a while the skin will loosen by itself.

SEASONED THISTLES

Thistles.—Lemon.—White pepper.—Garlic.—Cinnamon.—Saffron.—Fried bread.—Oil.—Flour.

The thistles should be white and tender. The green leaves should be removed and also the nerves of the leaves. Cut them in pieces of two inches or more. Cook them in boiling water with a squirt of lemon (1). Place salt, a pinch of white pepper, cinnamon and garlic which has been previously mashed in the mortar with a piece of fried bread and a pinch of saffron, in a frying pan with oil and fry lightly. Add a tsp. of flour to thicken the sauce. Pour this sauce on top of the thistles and allow to cook for a moment, adding a little bit more of the water in which they were cooked in the beginning, if necessary.

SPINACH

Spinach is cooked in the same way as cabbage. It is used to garnish some meat or egg dishes.

---

(1) When they are cooked, drain the water and keep it for later use.

STEWED BRUSSEL SPROUTS

Brussel sprouts.—Butter.—Ham.—Salt.—Flour.

Wash Brussel sprouts with cold water and place them to cook in boiling water. When they are almost cooked add enough salt to season since they are almost saltless. Let them cook for another five minutes stirring them well since they contain a lot of earth and after this time drain them.

Melt the butter and add some flour to thicken it. Add a little bit of the water in which the Brussel sprouts were cooked, then the ham (finely chopped) and the Brussel sprouts. Let them cook for another 15 minutes and they are ready to be served.

The Brussel sprouts can also be cooked with onion, garlic, tomato, etc. as you do with the meat.

Once they are cooked they can be served also with sauce «bechamel», sprinkled with grated cheese, and placed in the oven.

Brussel sprouts are used to garnish meats, along with peas, cauliflower, etc.

STEWED LENTILS

Lentils.—Onion.—Garlic.—Parsley.—Oil.—Lemon if desired.

Soak them overnight and place them to cook when the water is boiling. Add onion, parsley and a clove of garlic without peeling but clean. Once they are cooked, add a bit of paprika fried in oil, and a squirt of lemon. Another variation is to add the onion, garlic, parsley, spices, etc. fried in oil when the lentils are half cooked, with a squirt of lemon.

In adition you may put pieces of fried ham, fried bread, «chorizo», etc.

STRING BEANS

String beans.—Salt.

The most tender of the string beans are the ones that are smooth and where the beans can not abviously be felt by running the finger lightly along the bean. The older beans will be more fibrous than the younger beans and with them it may be necessary to remove the hard fiber or hilum on both sides of the sheath. When this is done, cut the beans into three pieces, and place them in salted boiling water.

The water in which the string beans have been cooked, is very nutritious and should be saved for later use either as a soup or a sauce.

Season the drained string beans with garlic, paprika and a squirt of lemon fried in oil.

They can also be covered with «sauce bechamel». Put them on a tray and place them for a few minutes in a hot oven.

A delicious variation could consist of string beans cooked with stewed potatoes. The beans can also be used as a garnish for various meat dishes, vegetables, etc.

STUFFED EGGPLANTS

Eight small eggplants.—One egg.—One fifth pound of hazelnuts and pine cone seeds.—One half pound of chopped meat (veal, pork, chicken, etc.).—A piece of salted ham.—Oil.—Salt.—Onion.—One half tbls. of grated cheese.—One tbls. of butter.

Wash the eggplants well and part them into two pieces. Place them in salted water for half an hour, and after this time remove the central meaty section for later use.

In oil fry the onion and half a clove of garlic chopped, the meat, the ham, and the meat you remove from the eggplant, all of this seasoned with salt. These ingredients are only lightly fried and the mixture is then used to stuff the shells of the eggplants. Top it with a few balls of butter and place them in the oven to bake for a few minutes.

Fry more chopped onion in oil, add the hazelnuts and pine cone seeds crushed and mix this with some water without salt. Leave to cook for twenty minutes, drain it and pour the liquid over the filled eggplants. Sprinkle the eggplants with grated cheese and place them in the oven for 30 minutes or more if necessary.

50

They should be served juicy but not with an excess of sauce.

STUFFED PIMIENTOS

Servings: 6

One large green pepper per person.—3 hard boiled eggs.—2 tbls. of bread crumbs.—One onion.—Salt and pepper to taste.—2 tbls. of butter.—One raw egg.—2 cups of tomato sauce.—A piece of ham.— A branch of parsley.

For the stuffing, chop the onion and parsley and fry these ingredients in butter with diced ham. Add the bread crumbs, the hard boiled eggs chopped and when this is well cooked, remove it from the fire. Allow it to cool a little, add the beaten raw egg and then season with salt and pepper. Cut off the stalk end of the peppers, fill them with the stuffing and to seal the end, you can brush it with a bit of beaten egg and sprinkle it with bread crumbs.

Place the stuffed peppers in a buttered oven pan, pour the tomato sauce over them and bake them in the oven for about an hour.

STUFFED ZUCCHINI SQUASH

Zucchini squash is cooked similarly to potatoes.

6 small squash.—One quarter pound of chopped meat (veal, pork, chicken, etc.).—One tbls. of chopped ham.—Onion.—Garlic.—Parsley.—Tomato.—One tbls. of almonds, hazelnuts, or walnuts.—One tbls. of grated cheese.—One egg.—Oil.—Flour.

In a small amount of oil, fry the chopped meat, the ham, garlic and parsley finely chopped, and after five minutes add a tomato without the skin and seeds and season this with salt. Remove it from the fire, add a beaten egg and mix all ingredients well.

51

The squash es are peeled and hollowed out similar to «Stuffed Potatoes» or you can cut them in two and hollow them out. With the stuffing previously made, fill the squash.

Fry well in hot oil the chopped onion, add a tbls. of flour and the almonds or hazelnuts (these should be mashed well in a mortar with a small amount of water). Allow these ingredients to boil for a minute and pour this mixture over the filled squash. Let them cook adding some water if necessary. Once they are cooked place them on a tray; the liquid is passed through the blender and then used to pour over the squash. Sprinkle with grated cheese and place in the oven for 10 minutes.

THISTLES WITH HAM

One big thistle.—One quarter pound of salted ham.— Oil.—Milk.—Lemon.—Flour.

The thistle should be white and tender. Remove the green leaves and the hard fibers from the stem. Thistles are cooked in the same way as cabbage. Cut the thistle into small pieces. Mix one tbls. of flour with a little water and add it to the thistles along with two small cups of hot stock until the water covers the thistles. Sprinkle it with lemon juice and stir it for a few minutes to avoid the thistles from sticking to the bottom. Cut the ham into small pieces, fry it lightly adding to it one tbls. of flour and a big cup of boiling milk, stirring it well.

When the thistles are cooked, drain them and place them with the ham and milk letting them cook for a few minutes.

Serve it garnished with strips of pimientos, thin French fries, etc.

THISTLES WITH WHITE SAUCE

One pound of thistles.—Oil.—Lemon.—One egg.— Flour.—Salt.—Garlic.—Walnuts.—Saffron.

Clean the thistles as in the former recipe and boil the pieces in water seasoned with salt and a squirt of lemon to prevent the thistles from getting black. Cook for more than half an hour until it is tender. Drain it, dip it into flour and beaten egg and place the pieces in an earthenware pan.

In a little bit of hot oil, fry a small amount of onion very well chopped with a tbls. of flour and start to add to this mixture half of the water in which the thistles were cooked and the same amount of milk.

In a mortar, mash a pinch of saffron previously roasted on a hot plate, one half a clove of garlic, one big walnut and a pinch of salt for the final seasoning. Add this mixture to the sauce and pour it over the thistles. Cover them up and let them cook for 10 minutes in the oven or on a hot plate with high heat. Serve it hot.

VEGETABLE «MENESTRA»

One pound of peas.—Three regular carrots.—Two pounds of artichokes.—Two or three potatoes.—One half pound of broad beans.—Onion.—Parsley.—Salt. Oil.—Lemon.

The carrots, peas, artichokes and broad beans are cooked in boiling water seasoned with salt and a squirt of lemon.

The peeled potatoes are diced and fried along with a chopped small onion. Mix this with the other drained vegetables, let it cook for a moment and serve it hot.

VEGETABLE PIE

Two pounds of cabbage.—Tomato.—A piece of salted ham or «chorizo».—Two eggs.—Salt.—Onion.—Garlic.—Oil.—Three or four tbls. of bread crumbs.— Sauce «bechamel».

Clean and chop the cabbage cooking it in boiling water with some salt. When it is cooked, drain it and place it in a deep tray. Fry in oil a small amount of chopped onion, garlic and the ham or «chorizo», then add a big tomato peeled and without seeds. Drain the cabbage again and mix it with the oil mixture, two beaten eggs and two or three tbls. of bread crumbs. Mix thoroughly and place it in a mold that has been buttered and sprinkled with bread crumbs. Place it in a double boiler or in the oven until the egg curdles, then empty it upside-down on a tray and when ready to serve pour on top the sauce «bechamel».

VEGETABLE PUDDING

Servings: 6

One cabbage of about two pounds.—Any other kind of vegetable (it is recomended to use green ones since they contain more vitamins than the white ones).— One half pound of meat (kidney, chicken, ham, or other kinds). — Onion. — Garlic. — Parsley. —Salt.— Stock or water.—Bread crumbs.—Sauce «bechamel».

Wash and part the vegetables and cook them in boiling water or stock with salt. The meat, a little bit of onion, one branch of parsley and half a clove of garlic, all finely chopped, are fried in a pan, first the meat and later the rest. If the meat is fried with the rest of the ingredients at the same time, it will cook but will not get brown as when fried. Season with salt.

When the vegetables are cooked, drain them well since they contain lots of water and mix them with the sauce prepared in advance. When everything is mixed, place it in a mold which has been previously buttered and sprinkled with bread crumbs. Empty it on a round tray by turning it upside-down and pour some sauce «bechamel» on top. The sauce should be very hot and not too thick. Serve immediately.

ZUCCHINI SQUASH WITH CARROTS

The best Zucchini squashes are the tender and small ones.

A few small and tender squashes.—Onion.—Tomato.—Carrots.—Salt.—White wine.—One egg.—Soft part of bread.—Chopped meat or chicken.

Scrape the squashes with a knife and hollow them out carefuly with a teaspoon. Wash them and stuff them with the chopped meat and onion. Cover the hole with the soft part of the bread dipped in beaten egg. Fry the squashes lightly in a casserole, adding chopped onion, tomato without seeds, one carrot (all these ingredients chopped), salt, one half cup of white wine and the necessary water to cook.

When they are cooked, drain the sauce and pour the liquid on top of the squashes. The carrot serves to garnish the serving tray.

Sauces and Garnishes

Sauces accompany almost all the dishes and they contribute to make the dishes more appetizing and exquisite.

Garnishes are called, in culinary terms, solid foods which are used to ornament dishes and at the same time contribute to the abundance of the dishes. There are many varieties of garnishes, among them are potatoes, fresh vegetables, carrots, beets, radishes, etc.

We can not possibly list the garnishes that can be used for every dish, but in many cases we suggest along with the recipe which one we think is best.

ALMOND SAUCE

One ounce of raw almonds.—One tbls. of flour.—Butter.—Onion.—Salt.—Nutmeg if desired.—Stock.

Fry the onion, finely chopped, in two or three tbls. of butter and a add one tbls. of flour pinch of nutmeg if you like. After stirring it for a minute, add two or three cups of stock or boiling water and the peeled almonds mashed.

Almonds are peeled after leaving them for a few minutes in boiling water. Stir continously for ten minutes and season with salt. Pass the sauce through the sieve and it is then ready to use.

BEETS FOR GARNISHING

One beet.—Cinnamon.—One pickle in vinegar.— Lemon.—Salt.

Place the peeled beet cut in large slices to cook in boiling water. Season it with a little cinnamon, other spices if you like, a quirt of lemon and a chopped pickle. When the beet is cooked and seasoned with salt, drain it and place it on the tray you desire.

You can also cook it in water, drain it and season it with raw oil, lemon and salt.

Beets prepared in this way are used to garnish meat and fish.

EGGPLANTS AND ZUCCHINI SQUASH

Eggplants contain vitamins B and C and such minerals as iron and magnesium. They are excellent for garnishing and they can be prepared as in the recipe given previously titled «Fried eggplants».

Zucchini squashes.—Butter.—Stock.—Onion.—Garlic.—Parsley.—Salt.—Laurel.

Peel the squashes and cut them in slices or pieces. Place them to cook in stock or boiling water in which you put pieces of onion, a few branches of parsley, a small leaf of laurel and season with salt.

Drain the water from the squashes, dry them and fry them in butter.

They are principally used to garnish various meats.

FISH SAUCE

Pieces of fish (head, intestins, skin, etc.).—White wine.—Leeks or a piece of onion.—Half a pound of tomatoes.—A few tbls. of butter.—Lemon.—Parsley.—Salt.—Pepper if you like.—One tbls. of flour.—Oil if desired.

When the pieces of fish have been cleaned and washed well, cook them in water. Chop finely the leek or onion. In the butter and a little oil, stir in a tbls. of flour, the chopped leek or onion, a pinch of pepper half a cup of white wine and place this to cook for a few minutes. When everything is well fried add the parted tomatoes without seeds, the parsley chopped and a squirt of lemon. Again leave it to cook for a few minutes. The fish is drained and the stock is added to the previous mixture. Leave to cook until it obtains the consistency desired. Sieve the sauce and serve it hot.

FRIED POTATOES

Good quality potatoes.—Oil.—Salt.

Peel and wash the potatoes, then cut them into thin slices. After salting them lightly add them to abundant hot oil a few at a time to avoid them from sticking. They are called English Style Potatoes, similar to potato chips.

They can also be cut in strips (similar to French fries) and fry them slowly to prevent them from getting too dark before being completely cooked through.

There are apparatuses available which cut potatoes into various patterns but the frying procedure is the same.

All potatoes have to be fried in abundant oil and a few at a time. It may be neccesary to sprinkle them with salt again.

GARNISHES FOR MEAT

Meats can be garnished with potato balls, mashed potatoes, fried potatoes mushrooms, stuffed tomatoes, lettuce, salads, carrots, artichokes, peas, asparagus, Brussel sprouts, etc.

GELATIN FOR FISH

Scraps of fish.—Gelatin.—One small carrot.—A bit of onion.—One leek.—Half a quart of water.—One egg white.

The fish, onion, carrot, and leek are placed to cook in water for 20 minutes to half an hour. The gelatin is dissolved in hot water and it is then added to the other ingredients which are boiling. After three minutes filter everything through a wet cloth. Add a beaten egg white, allow to boil for a moment, filter it again and it is then ready to use.

GELATIN FOR MEAT OR FOWL

Two quarts of water.—One half pound of beef.—One leg of veal or pork.—One half pound of carrots.— Two egg whites.

Cook the meats and carrots for three or four hours. Remove from fire and drain it through a sieve. Let it cool, mix the beaten egg whites without letting them curdle and let it boil for a few minutes. Skim it, put it through the sieve and let it cool.

GOOSEBERRY SAUCE

For stewed or roasted game, especially big game.

The juice from three large lemons.—One cup of the juice from the roast or stew.—«Onion sauce».— «Tomato sauce».—One tbls. of butter.—Two tbls. of gooseberry concentrate.

Mix the lemon juice and the juice from the meat and allow it to boil until the liquid is reduced to half its volume.

Then you add one half cup of «Onion sauce», another half cup of «Tomato sauce», one tbls. of butter, and the two tbls. of gooseberry concentrate. Mix it well and let it boil for a minute. Season with salt, pass it through the sieve and then it is ready to be used.

GREEN SAUCE

Two tbls. of flour.—Oil.—Onion.—Parsley.—Salt.— Garlic.—Stock.

Brown the flour lightly in oil and add a tbls. of chopped onion mashed in a mortar. When the onion is browned add one cup of stock, season with salt and let it boil.

Mash a few branches of parsley with a little water and mix them with the other ingredients. Then it is ready to serve. Use with fish and vegetables.

HIGHLY SEASONED SAUCE

«Madeira sauce».—Lemon.—Some cucumbers and capers.

When the «Madeira sauce» is made, add the chopped cucumbers and capers with a squirt of lemon. This sauce is used with pork, cold meats and fowl.

MADEIRA SAUCE

Pork lard.—Butter.—Flour.—Salt.—Concentrated stock.—Madeira wine (dry wine).

Using pork and beef lard in equal proportion, fry one tbls. of flour per two tbls. of lard. When the flour is browned add per every tbls. of flour one small glassful of wine and one tbls. of concentrated stock, allowing it to cook for a while. Season with salt if necessary.

MASHED POTATOES «DUQUESA»

One pound of potatoes.—One tbls. of butter.—Milk.—Salt.—One egg.

Wash the potatoes without peeling them and place them to cook in boiling water. When they are cooked and drained, peel them immediately since they get hard when they cool. Mash them with the blender and place them in a casserole containing the melted butter and some milk. This casserole should be kept warm all the time. Beat the egg, mix it with the mashed potatoes and season with salt.

The consistency desired can be obtained by adding more or less milk. If the mashed potatoes are rather thick, you can make small balls and fry them. They are used as garnish for meats principally.

MAYONNAISE SAUCE

The mayonnaise sauce is used with fish, seafood, eggs, vegetables, etc.

One egg yolk.—One small glass of refined oil.—Lemon.—Salt.

The egg and the oil should be at room temperature. If they are cold, the mayonnaise will curdle. This sauce is very delicate and if it is not beaten well it will curdle easily. First you beat the yolk and when it is beaten add very slowly (almost drop by drop) the oil, beating continuously. A smaller amount of oil may be used if you do not wish so much sauce but you should never use a bigger amount than indicated in the recipe.

At the end add very carefully the salt and a squirt of lemon. The amount of salt and lemon is up to the individual since tastes vary.

If you see that the mayonnaise starts to curdle, add a few drops of cold water stirring it continuously. It could happen that in spite of this, the mayonnaise still will curdle, then you should start by beating another egg yolk, adding the former curdled mayonnaise instead of oil.

The consistency of the mayonnaise can be reduced by adding milk to it. To make the mayonnaise last longer you must add very slowly a small amount of gelatin previously disolved in water.

MUSHROOMS FOR GARNISHING

Mushrooms.—Onion.—Lemon.—Flour.—Oil or butter.—Salt.

Wash the mushrooms and cut them into pieces. Fry them lightly in oil or butter, sprinkle with flour and after stirring momentarily season with salt and add a squirt of lemon. After stirring them again they are ready to be used.

MUSHROOM SAUCE

One half pound of mushrooms.—One tbls. of pork lard.—A squirt of oil.—One big cup of «Tomato Sauce».—Two tbls. of concentrated stock.—A small glass of white wine.—One half ounce of brandy.—Salt.

Melt the lard with the oil in a casserole. Wash the mushrooms, dry them with a cloth and chop them very finely. Fry them lightly in the oil and lard, then you add the «Tomato sauce», the concentrated stock, the wine and the brandy. Season with salt and let it boil for a few minutes until the liquid thickens a little. Then it is ready to use. This sauce is mainly used to garnish meats.

ONION SAUCE

One half quart of stock.—Two tbls. of flour.—A small carrot.—A small onion.—Salt.—Garlic.—Oil.—One ounce of «tocino».

Fry the chopped «tocino» in a little oil. When it is almost fried add the chopped carrot, onion in small pieces and half of a clove of garlic finely chopped. When everything is lightly brown add the flour, stir for a few moments and pour the mixture on the stock leaving it cook for 15 or 20 minutes. When it is cooked pass it through the sieve and use it.

POTATOES «A LA VITORIA»

Potatoes.—Oil.—Salt.

Peel the potatoes and cut them into long and thick pieces. Season with salt and fry them in abundant oil not too hot so they do not get burned. When they are light brown remove them from the oil. They are used to garnish meats.

PRAWN SAUCE

A few prawns.—White wine.—One egg yolk.—Butter.—Onion.—Parsley.—Salt.—Flour.

Cook the prawns in a little bit of water to which you add a squirt of white wine, a branch of parsley, a few pieces of onion and salt. When they are cooked, separate the tails from the rest of the bodies and peel the tails. Reserve the tails for later use. The rest of the bodies are mashed in the mortar, mixed with the water in which they were cooked and allowed to cook again for a few minutes.

In one tbls. of butter, fry lightly one tsp. of flour per every small cup of liquid.

Drain the liquid and pass it through a wet cloth. To this liquid add the flour with butter let it boil for five minutes and season with salt. Remove from fire and add one egg yolk mixing it well with the sauce. Add the tails and the sauce is ready to be used. The prawn sauce is used with fish.

SAUCE «AL AJO ARRIERO»

Garlic.—Lemon.—Oil.—Salt.

Mash the garlic in a mortar, add a little lemon and a good amount of refined oil. Season with salt. The amounts of lemon and salt depend on the taste of the cook. Stir it well.

SAUCE «ALI-OLI»

«Mayonnaise sauce».—Garlic.

When the «Mayonnaise sauce» is prepared, add the garlic very well chopped.

SAUCE «BECHAMEL»

This sauce is used along with meats, fish, eggs, vegetables and all kinds of dishes.

One half quart of milk.—Two or three tbls. of flour.— Two or three tbls. of butter or oil.—Salt.

Fry the flour very lightly in oil or butter. Per every tbls. of flour use two tbls. of oil or a bigger amount if you are using butter.

When the flour has been very lightly fried, start to add the milk stirring it and allowing it to cook. The consistency of the sauce can be regulated as always by adding more or less milk.

This sauce must be served very hot because if it cools, it gets quite thick.

SAUCE FOR CHICKPEAS

One egg.—One onion.—Bread.—Lemon.—Stock.— Oil.

Fry a piece of bread in hot oil. When it is lightly brown, mash it in the mortar, add to it one tbls. of lemon juice, a chopped hard boiled egg and a small cup of stock. If you want a thicker sauce do not add so much stock. Season with salt. Pass it through the sieve and add it to the chickpeas.

SAUCE FOR EVERYTHING

One cup of stock.—The juice from three big lemons.— A midium cup of white wine.—Spices if desired.— One clove.—A pinch of pepper.—Salt.—A piece of an orange rind.—Laurel.

Place all these ingredients in a casserole or in a glass container. Once they are mixed and seasoned with salt, place them in a cool place for 12 or 14 hours. Pass the mixture through the sieve and keep it in a bottle well closed. It lasts for a long time.

SAUCE FOR FISH

Stock.—White wine.—Pepper.—Salt.—Lemon.— Laurel.—Garlic.—Parsley.

5

Mix one half cup of stock, a small squirt of white wine, a pinch of pepper, a slice or rinds from a lemon, a small leaf of laurel, a branch of parsley, one half clove of garlic, and the salt necessary. Heat the mixture and let it stand in a warm place for 6 or 7 hours.

To use, fry a tsp. of flour in a little oil and add the mixture previously prepared and sieved.

SAUCE FOR ROASTS

Butter.—Onion.—Parsley.—Salt.—Lemon.—Stock.

This sauce is placed on the tray or in the casserole in which you are going to make the roast. First add the butter, next the chopped onion and parsley, a small amount of stock, a squirt of lemon and season it with salt. Place the roast in this sauce and puit it in the oven. Occasionally scoop the sauce over the roast.

SAUCE «MAITRE D'HOTEL»

Principally used for fish.

Butter.—Parsley.—Pepper.—Salt.

Place the butter in a cup and mix it with chopped parsley, a small amount of pepper and season it with salt. To mix it use a wooden spoon previously dipped in water to prevent the butter from sticking.

Spread the serving tray with the butter mixture, then place the tray on top of a container with boiling water so that the butter may melt. Place the prepared meal on the tray and serve it with lemon juice.

For white fish, the sauce can be thickend with an egg yolk.

STRAWBERRY SAUCE

Strawberries.—Sugar.

Using equals amounts of strawberries and sugar, add one tbls. of water per quarter pound of sugar. Allow to cook for ten minutes, put it through the blender and when it is cold use it for icecream, sweet.

TARTAR SAUCE

This sauce goes well with potatoes and fish.

«Mayonnaise sauce».—Olives.—Seasoned pickles.— Mustard.—Parsley.—Capers if desired.

In the mayonnaise sauce add chopped olives, pickles, parsley, a pinch of mustard and the other ingredient if desired. Everything must be chopped and mixed well and you may add more of whatever ingredients you like best.

This sauce is used cold.

TOMATO SAUCE

Oil.—Tomatoes.—Salt.—Onion.

Place the tomatoes in hot water for a few seconds, remove them, dry them and then peel. Cut them through horizontally, remove the seeds and fry them lightly in hot oil, seasoning with salt. Add some pieces of onion and continue frying for a few minutes.

If you want to use the tomatoes without peeling them, you can cook them but add a little bit of sugar to neutralize the acid which comes mainly from the seeds. When cooking the tomatoes with the skin it is necessary to sieve the sauce before using it.

Garlic and spices may be added to give more flavour.

TRUFFLE SAUCE

Two or more tbls. of butter.—One tbls. of flour.— One small can of truffles.—Salt.

Fry the flour in butter very lightly. Chop the truffles and mix them with the butter and flour, seasoning with salt. Leave it to cook with a little bit of water.

VINEGAR SAUCE

This sauce is used for salads and boiled fish.

Garlic.—Lemon.—Onion.—Parsley.—Oil.—Salt.

The onion is chopped very finely along with a few branches of parsley and garlic. Add refined oil and a squirt of lemon. Season it with salt mixed in a small amount of water, stirring it continously and cooking it until it is of the desired consistency. When the sauce is to be served, you may add any of the following ingredients very well chopped: hard boiled egg, pickles, olives, etc.

ZUCCHINI SQUASH FOR GARNISHING

Zucchini squashes.—Butter.—Stock.—Onion.—Garlic.—Parsley.—Salt.—Laurel.

Clean and peel the Zucchini squashes and cut them into slices or pieces.

Cook them in the stock or boiling water in which you have previously added pieces of onion, branches of parsley, a small leaf of laurel and season with salt.

When they are cooked (tender) fry them in butter after they have been drained and dried.

Use them to accompany meats and roasts principally.

Fries, pastes and various dishes

BAKED «CANELONES»

«Canelones».—Chopped meat (fish, ham, fowl, etc. may also be used).—Onion.—Garlic.—Parsley.—Tomato.—Oil.—Sauce «bechamel».—Grated cheese.

Buy the «canelones». They are rectangular sheets of white paste presented in small boxes. The paste is similar to the one of macaroni.

Place them in boiling water and allow to cook for 10 minutes being careful not to soften them too much. When they are cooked take them out of the water with a skimmer and place them on a cloth to dry.

You can also make «canelones» at home with milk, flour, salt and an egg white forming a thick batter. After it is well kneaded, form thin sheets and cut small rectangles, proceeding with them in the same way as with the bought ones.

The onion, garlic, parsley and tomato, are chopped and mixed with the meat. This mixture is fried lightly and it is placed on the rectangles. Roll these and form tubes which you put on an earthenware tray. Pour some sauce «bechamel» on top, sprinkle with cheese and leave them in the oven for a few minutes.

BAKED MUSHROOMS

One half pound of mushrooms.—Bread crumbs.—Refined oil.—Parsley.—Stock.—White wine.—Lemon.

Wash the mushrooms well since they contain a lot of earth. Drain them upsidedown and dry them, then place them on a tray in the same way and sprinkle with salt. Next, you sprinkle them abundantly with bread crumbs, chopped parsley, refined oil, stock and a squirt of white wine or lemon juice. Place them in the oven until they are cooked, watching once in a while to add more stock if necessary, so that the mushrooms do not dry. If you get sick from eating poisonous mushrooms or mushrooms in bad condition, eat honey or a tbls. of raw brains or liver from a rabbit as soon as you feel the first symptoms of poisoning since it has been proved that these foods contain the antivenin.

BRAINS PUDDING

Calf brains.—Chard, spinach or any other kind of fine vegetable.—Carrots.—Four eggs.—Buter.—Pepper.—Bread crumbs.—Onion.—Garlic.—Sauce «bechamel», «White sauce», or another.—White wine.

Wash, chop the vegetables and place them to cook in boiling water with a piece of onion, garlic and the carrots peeled and washed.

Prepare two hard boiled eggs.

Wash the brains in cold water removing the fine skin that wraps them and place them to cook in boiling water with a few pieces of onion, garlic, parsley, a squirt of white wine and seasoned with salt or a squirt of lemon.

When the vegetables are cooked, drain them well, season

them with salt and mix them well with two beaten eggs, a piece of butter and the pepper if desired.

The cooked brains are drained, placed on a cutting board and cut into thin slices.

Place layers of vegetables, brains and slices of hard boiled eggs in a mold previously buttered and sprinkled with bread crumbs. Allow to cook in a double boiler for 10 minutes.

Empty the mold and cover it with sauce «bechamel», «white sauce» or any other.

«CALLOS A LA MADRILEÑA»

Servings: 6

About two pounds of tripe.—Lemon.—One quarter cup of vinegar.—About three normal carrots.—Two tbls. marjoram.—One half cup of oil.—Two leeks.— One glassful of white wine.—Four slices of bacon.— One «chorizo».—One leaf of laurel.—Three tbls. of ketchup or tomato sauce.—A couple branches of parsley.—Two cups of stock.—Three tbls. of rock salt.—One sliced onion.—One onion well chopped.— One cup of sherry.—One pork foot.—One dozen pepper corns.—Two cloves of chopped garlic.—Salt.

Clean the tripe well in several sets of water. Next rub the tripe with the lemon and then the rock salt. When this has been done, leave the tripe to soak in water containing the vinegar for half an hour and this water is then discarded. The tripe is then boiled in fresh water for about fifteen minutes and drained.

To the tripe you now add, the pork foot split lengthwise, the chopped garlic, the sliced onion, the carrots chopped, parsley, seasoning, one cup of sherry, one glassful of white wine, and the stock. All this is brought to boiling point and then simmered for about three hours.

When it has cooled, the tripe is cut into square pieces and the meat from the pork foot is removed and diced.

In a saucepan you now fry in oil, the chopped onion, sliced bacon and «chorizo». When this has fried for a few minutes, add the tripe, pork meat, tomatoes and pepper corns. The ingredients are browned very slowly and then placed in an earthenware dish. The liquid in which the tripe was cooked is poured over everything and it is simmered again for about two hours.

CROQUETTES

Oil.—Flour.—Salt.—Chopped meat, ham, fish, etc.— Bread crumbs.—One egg.

Fry the oil with garlic, bread, rinds of orange, etc. to take away any flavour the oil could have. In this oil, after removing the other ingredients, fry very lightly four tbls. of flour. Do not let the flour get brown. To the oil and flour, add very slowly half a quart of cold milk stirring continously to prevent the cold milk from sticking to the bottom. Add milk until you get a thick cream. This cream or sauce is like sauce «bechamel» but much thicker. Let it boil for 15 minutes stirring continously.

Fry the chopped meat lightly in oil and add it to the cream when it is cooked. Mix it well, extend it on a tray previously wet with cold water, and let it cool.

Beat two eggs and on a different plate put the bread crumbs. When the paste is cold, take big spoonfuls, dip them in egg, then in the bread crumbs and fry them in abundant oil. While frying, turn them so that they get fried evenly. Drain them well from the oil and place them on a serving tray.

«EMPANADA MALLORQUINA»

One pound of flour.—Two tbls. of pork lard.—Half a wine glass of refined oil.—Half a wine glass of water.—One or two egg yolks.—Three quarters of a pound of meat (pork, lamb, etc.).—One regular orange.—White paper.

parsley a   l
add the   (
seeds and   i
time will   s

SOFT Bl   N

Br
wil
Oi

Clean   s
and cook   b
branches   s
without p   f
or a squir   y
salt.   a
    Beat t   t
and then   I
necessary   n
a rather
by bit.
    When   N
on a boar
dipped in
    Fry a
the lemor
The lemo   a
brains wh   ti
the oil ov   T
to puff ur
brief) rem   is
place then   p
    sa
    ir

SPAGHE

    Spaghe   N
a la Italiai
given for
    cc

Mix the water, oil, orange juice, the egg yolks, and a good pinch of salt. When everything is mixed, add the flour slowly mixing it with a spoon or with your fingers but without kneading it.

Prepare the meat as you wish. Roll two thirds of the dough out on a sheet of thick white paper and place the meat on top of the dough. Roll the other third of the dough out as well and use it to cover the meat.

Fold the lower edges over the top dough edge and pinch together to close firmly. Brush the dough with egg white and place it in the oven to bake for half an hour at medium heat.

EMPANADILLA

Equal amounts of water, white wine and oil.—Salt.— One half tsp. of yeast powder.—Flour.—Filling.

Mix the water, wine, oil, yeast and add enough salt so that the mixture is rather salty. Add enough flour to form a paste that when kneaded is not hard. Let this dough stand in a warm place for half an hour.

After this time roll the dough out and cut it into circles with a glass or rectangles. Place one tsp. of filling on each piece of dough, place another piece of dough on the top and pinch the edges together. The filling can be made of a mixture with meat, fish, hard boiled egg, etc. previously prepared.

Fry them in abundant hot oil, sprinkling the hot oil on top with a skimmer. Do not flip the «empanadillas» as the sprinkling of the oil allows the top surface to puff and brown.

Another variation is to fill them with sweet cream.

FROG HAUNCHES

The best frog season is from March to May. When the frog legs are washed and peeled, soak them for one hour in equal parts of water and milk to soften them. After this time they are drained and dried with a cloth.

served
for a f

ROA

Wi
not sti
Plɛ
on to
with g
pressu
this ti
and tł
top of
into tł
or colɛ

SNAI

Th
snails
all the
days.
place
salt fo
After
are pɛ
snails
warm
inside
Plɛ

STUFFED «BIZCOCHO»

One yellow sponge cake, «bizcocho».—Chopped meat, fish, etc.—Sauce «bechamel».—«Tomato sauce» or other.

Make a sponge cake of your preference containing no sugar and a little bit of salt and make it in a square or circular shape. Cut it horizontally in half. Make a filling with chopped meat, fish, etc. and tomato sauce or other sauce if desired. The filling is previously cooked and it is then placed between the two layers of cake. When it is ready to serve, place it on a tray and cover it with sauce «bechamel». The sauce should be very hot and not too thick.

«TOURNEDOS A LA AMERICANA»

«Tournedos» are thick slices of beef. The best meat to be used is loin. They are cooked similar to fillets.

Roasted meat or sirloin fillets.—Slices of salted ham.— Eggs.—Tomato sauce.—Slices of bread.—Oil.

Cut the bread in slices and fry them quickly in hot oil, drain them well. Fry also the salted ham with some fat on it. The roasted meat is cut into slices or if you are using the sirloin fillets, fry them.

On top of each slice of bread, place one slice of meat or fillet, one slice of ham and a fried egg. Cover everything with «tomato sauce» and place in the oven for 5 minutes. Serve hot. Add the juice from the roasted meat to the sauce. Asparagus may be used for garnishing.

«VOL-AU-VENT»

«Hojaldre» (This recipe is given under the chapter of «Cakes and Pastries»).—Meats or seafood for filling.

With the dough to make «hojaldre», form a round shape mass of the size of a plate. When this has been done,

78

use a glass or any other object of circular shape to mark a circunference in the center part of the dough. Place in the oven to cook with not too much heat since the «hojaldre» is very delicate and burns easily. The dough will be about an inch thick. Prepare the filling as you wish using seafood, meat, fish, ham, hard boiled eggs, vegetables, or any other ingredient you like.

When the «hojaldre» is cooked remove the circumference previously marked and hollow the cake a little bit more if necessary. Stuff the cake with the filling, cover it with the part removed and serve.

continously, and then add the water which you have boiled previously (it must be hot). Add the saffron, crushed in a mortar and salt to taste, stirring everything to mix well. Cook the «paella» on high fire for about five minutes, and then turn the heat down to moderate for 10 to 15 minutes. The seafood is added when the rice is half cooked. Since the artichokes and peas are canned, they should be added about five minutes before cooking is completed. More water may have to be added as the «paella» cooks.

From the point of adding the seafood, the «paella» should not be stirred, only shook slightly occasionally to prevent the rice from sticking. A squirt of lemon mixed with the water being used, will prevent the rice from sticking.

The water in which the seafood is cooked and also the juice from any other ingredients, should be used before it is necessary to use tap water.

The peppers can be cut into strips and used to decorate as well as sliced hard boiled eggs.

Allow the «paella» to rest for 5 minutes after cooking before serving.

RICE «A LA ITALIANA»

«White rice» (This is the basic ingredient for several rice dishes and its preparation can be found at the end of this chapter).

Tomato sauce.—Grated cheese.—Butter.

Mix the white rice with the tomato sauce. On a plate or oven tray put a coat of rice, spreadit with butter, then grated cheese. Repeat again with a layer or rice, butter and cheese. Place it in the oven for a few minutes. Serve hot.

RICE «A LA MARINERA»

One pound of rice.—Small glass of white wine.— Clams.—Shrimps.—Any other kind of seafood if

desired.—Onion.—Garlic.—Parsley.—Two regular tomatoes.—Peppers.—Oil.—Salt.

The seafood is cleaned well and cooked in white wine mixed with water and seasoned with salt. The seafood should be covered with liquid so that in the cooking process it is cleaned. Stir the seafood while it is cooking and when it is done, drain it and allow the water to settle.

Clean and wash the rice. In hot oil, fry lightly a small amount of onion, garlic and parsley finely chopped, then add the tomato peeled and seeded. Next, add the rice, a few pieces of pimiento and stir briefly.

In a casserole place double amount of water than rice. This water should be the water in which the safood was cooked. If you need more water, use tap water or stock. Season this with salt before adding the rice, if necessary. The water must be boiling before adding the rice. Remove the shells from the seafood and add it to the rice, allowing it to cook for 10 minutes over a strong fire stirring continously. The rice is removed from the fire and allowed to rest for a few minutes. If the rice is not going to be eaten immediately, add a squirt of lemon to prevent the rice from sticking.

RICE PUDDING

«White rice» (recipe follows in this chapter).

Meat filling with tomato, etc.—Mayonnaise.

Mix the «white rice» with the meat filling previously prepared. Place it in the oven for a few minutes, so that the rice will absorb the meat flavor. Remove it from the oven and cover it with mayonnaise, after it has been molded and placed on a tray.

RICE SOUFFLÉ

One pound of «White rice» (recipe follows in this chapter).—Seasoned chopped meat, ham, kidneys, fowl or any other meat.—Two eggs.

When the «white rice» is prepared, make alternate layers of rice and meat mixture on a tray, finishing with the rice. The meat mixture is prepared with seasoned chopped meat, garlic, onion, tomato, etc.

Beat the egg whites until it stands in peaks. The egg yolks are beaten separately and when both are done, fold the beaten egg yolks together with the whipped egg whites. Cover the rice with this and place it in the oven for a minute until the egg is lightly browned.

STEWED RICE

This dish is prepared similar to «White rice» but adding paprika to taste. «Chorizo» and ham are chopped and added.

The recipe for «White rice» is given at the end of this chapter.

WHITE RICE

Onion.—Garlic.—Laurel.—Rice.—Salt.—Parsley.— Oil.

In oil, fry the onion, garlic and laurel, all in big pieces and then add the rice.

In a casserole put a double amount of water than rice and season with salt so that the water is a little salty. When the water is boiling, add the rice, onion, etc. Allow it to boil over strong fire for 5 minutes, stirring frequently. Cover the rice with this and place it in the oven for a minute it on a hot plate or in the oven under low heat for another 10 or 15 minutes. When it is cooked remove the onion, garlic and laurel.

This rice is used to accompany fried eggs, kidneys, squids in their own ink, etc.

Eggs and omelets

ASPARAGUS OMELET

> **Two eggs.—One quarter cup of olive oil.—Three or four tips of asparagus; these can be cooked, frozen or canned.—Salt to taste.**

If you are using fresh asparagus, boil them until they are tender. Cut the asparagus into pieces one inch long and heat them briefly in the olive oil. Let them cool before you add them to the two eggs, beaten with a pinch of salt. Now proceed as instructed in the recipe for «French omelet».

EGGS «AL PLATO»

Servings: 2

> **Four eggs.—One regular tomato chopped.—One small chopped onion.—One tbls. oil.—A few branches of chopped parsley.—A few slices of sausage.—Some grated cheese.—Salt and pepper to taste.**

When the onion has been fried until it is just transparent, add the tomato and cook this until it is tender. Grease the bottom of another casserole and then put the onion-tomato mixture in it. Next the eggs are broken on top of this and a slice of sausage placed next to each egg yolk. Everything is then sprinkled with the chopped parsley and grated chese. Bake it in the oven under moderate heat for about ten minutes, so that the egg whites are done but the egg yolks should be soft.

EGGS «A LA JARDINERA»

Eggs.—Ham.—Peas.—Potatoes.—Lettuce.—Onion. Salt.—Oil.—Stock.

In hot oil, fry diced ham and potatoes, peas, and lettuce and onion finely chopped. When everything is fried, add a small cup of stock and allow to cook. Season with salt.

The eggs can be poached, fried or prepared as in the recipe for «Eggs al plato». They also can be boiled and cut in four pieces, etc. Adorn the eggs with the sauce which contains potatoes, ham, etc. This dish may also be garnished with asparagus, radishes, artichoke hearts, etc.

EGGS «AU GRATIN»

Six eggs.—One half pound of spinach.—Sauce «bechamel».—Salt.—Lemon.—Grated cheese.— Chopped ham.—Oil.—Butter.—«Tartaletas de ho- jaldre» (the recipe for these, can be found in the chapter of «Cakes and Pastries»).

Cook the spinach in boiling water and salt. The recipe for «Sauce bechamel» can be found in the chapter of «Sauces and Garnishes».

In boiling water seasoned with salt and a squirt of lemon, add the broken eggs, let them curdle, take them out with a skimer, place them on a clean cloth, cover them up to dry and sprinkle them with salt.

86

Drain the spinach, cut it very well, add some grated cheese and chopped ham and fry this in butter or refined oil. Season it with salt and add it to the «sauce bechamel».

On the «tartaletas» put tsp. of this sauce and place them in the oven for a few moments so that the «tartaletas» get soft and take the flavour from the sauce.

Withdraw the «tartaletas» from the oven and place one egg inside of each one covering it with «sauce bechamel». Place a piece of butter on top of each egg, sprinkle with grated cheese and chopped ham and place them in the oven so that they do not get cold. Serve them hot.

EGGS «ENCAPOTADOS»

Eggs.—Canned tunafish, fowl or veal.—«Sauce bechamel».

The eggs are boiled and after they are cool, cut them in half. Reserve in each egg, half of the yolk for later use. The other half, mix it with the tunafisch and with this mixture fill the egg. Place the half eggs with the flat part on the bottom on an oven tray, cover them up with «sauce bechamel» and place them in the oven. To serve, sprinkle them with the yolk we reserved.

EGGS FLAMENCO STYLE

Servings: 3

One half dozen eggs.—One quarter cup of oil.— One half pound of «chorizos».—One half pound of chopped ham.—Six ounces of string beans cut into pieces.—One pound of peeled and chopped tomatoes.— One medium onion chopped.—One clove of garlic mashed in a mortar.—Half a cup of previously cooked or canned peas.

Preheat the oil in a frying pan and then add the onion and garlic, letting it fry until it is golden. The ham is added and cooked for 2 minutes, then the tomatoes which are cooked for about ten minutes. This is then seasoned with salt and pepper. The string beans, the peas, sausages are then added all finely sliced. This sauce is divided into three individual casseroles and the eggs are then broken over each individual serving. Put them in the oven and let them cook until the eggs are done.

EGGS IN NESTS

Bread.—Eggs.—Butter.—Oil.—Salt.—«Tomato sauce» or any other one.

Cut thick slices of bread and hollow them in the central part but not completely. In the hollow part, put a small piece of butter and a cracked egg with the yolk in the hole. Sprinkle with salt.

With a skimmer, place them in a big frying pan with abundant oil and sprinkle the oil over them until the egg whites set. Take them out carefully and place them on a tray. The eggs are accompanied by tomato sauce or any other sauce you like.

EGGS WITH «BECHAMEL»

Eggs.—«Tomato sauce».—«Sauce bechamel».— Butter.

Boil the eggs for 5 minutes. You may cut them lengthwise in two halfs or leave them whole. Place them on a layer of tomato sauce. The recipe for «bechamel» is found in the chapter of «Sauces and Garnishes».

Cover the eggs with «Sauce bechamel», sprinkle with small pieces of butter and place in the oven for 5 minutes under strong heat. Serve immediately.

EGGS WITH HAM

Eggs.—Thopped ham.—Bread.—Oil.—Salt.—Tomato sauce, salad or any other sauce to accompany the eggs.

Fry round slices of bread quickly so that they will not get hard and drain the oil from them. The chopped ham is fried lightly and placed on top of the bread. The eggs are fried or poached and placed on top of the ham.

A tomato sauce, a salad or any other sauce may serve as a garnish for the eggs.

FRENCH OMELET

One egg.—A little ham if wanted.—Salt.—Oil.— A branch of parsley.

Beat the egg and mix the parsley and chopped ham. If you are using ham, it will probably not be necessary to add salt. The parsley can be eliminated and two or more eggs can be used per serving.

You can fry the omelet in butter or in oil, but use very little so that the omelet will not be too greasy. The omelet is not made flat but instead it is rolled gradually as it cooks and it is best if it is a little tender in the center. Serve it hot.

FRIED EGGS

Eggs.—Oil.—Salt.

Crack the eggs in a cup or on a plate and sprinkle them with salt. Place the eggs carefully into a small frying pan containing enough oil that the eggs can float when frying. The oil should not be too hot so that the eggs would not bubble. The egg whites should fry little by little so that the egg yolks do not break and remain soft. When the eggs begin to set, the heat can be increased but not so that it creates bubbles. Drain the oil from the eggs and serve them hot.

MUSHROOM OMELET

Prepare a flat «French omelet» and separately fry some mushrooms in butter or prepare them like in the recipe

«Mushrooms for garnishing». The mushrooms are then placed in the center of the omelet and the edges are folded over. Place it on a hot plate and serve it immediately after cooking.

This omelet may be accompanied by a fresh salad.

POACHED EGGS

To prepare poached eggs, you simply crack them into boiling water with salt and allow them to set. It is more convenient if a small pot is used so that the egg white is not spread out, which makes a better presentation.

If preparing the eggs in a soup, the size of the pot does not matter as the egg whites can be trimmed if they spread too much.

POTATO OMELET

Two pounds of potatoes.—One big onion.—One clove of garlic.—One branch of parsley and ham if desired.—Three or four eggs.—Oil.—Salt.

Peel the potatoes, wash them and cut them in small pieces. At the same time chop the onion, clove of garlic, branch of parsley and ham. Mix everything, season with salt and put in a frying pan with abundant oil, very hot.

Stir the mixture until it is fried to prevent it from sticking to the bottom. In a deep tray beat the eggs and with a skimmer take the potatoes from the frying pan and add them to the eggs. When this is done, remove part of the oil in the frying pan and leave only the necessary to make the omelet.

Mix thoroughly the potatoes with the eggs and place the mixture in the frying pan allowing to brown first on one side. For this operation the fire should not be very strong. Then turn the omelet to the other side and fry for two minutes. If you like the omelet harder, fry it longer. This dish may be served hot or cold.

SHRIMP OMELET

Four eggs.—One third of a pound of shrimps.—Salt.—Oil.

Beat the eggs, peel the shrimps when raw, add them to the eggs and season with salt.

Pour the eggs and shrimps in a frying pan with a little bit of hot oil and allow the eggs to begin to set. Stir the mixture lightly with a fork to allow all the egg to set. When it is almost set, turn the omelet over the other side and let fry for a moment. The omelet should not be very hard. Serve it hot.

STEWED EGGS

Eggs.—Oil.—Salt.—Paprika.

Fry the eggs, draining the oil well. Sprinkle a pinch of paprika on top of the eggs and then a squirt of boiling oil. Serve them hot.

STEWED OMELET

Make a «Potato omelet» and then cook it in stock or water. The amount of the liquid to be used must be enough to cover the omelet at ease. Add a squirt of white wine and a few tomatoes if desired. It is done in about half an hour. The omelet is served with the liquid in which it cooked. If adding the tomatoes, pass them through the masher or blender first. Be careful when you remove the omelet from the casserole since it tends to break easily.

Fish

Fish contain almost the same chemical principles as meat and they are rich in vitamins but contain more water. It is important to give advise regarding the preservation of fish. If fish are not well kept and preserved, they will decompose easily, creating toxic substances for the human body. Fresh fish are recognized by the red colour of the gills, the clear and transparent eyes, the rigidity in many species, etc.

The digestibility of fish is greater in the species with a low content of grease, as hake, sole, sea bass, brill, etc.

Fish contain more calcium than meat, but due to their bigger content of water, at equal amounts, the fish is less nutritious.

Fish can be divided into three big families:

White fish. Those species with fine meat and easy digestion, are considered white fish. Among these species we can list some of them: Hake, sole, codling, codfish, angler, trout, grouper, tench, red surmullet, perch, sea bream, sturgeon, plaice, sea bass, dory, barb, etc.

Blue fish. They are a little tougher than white fish and of more difficult digestion. Among these are: Tunafish, sardine, salmon, tuna, lamprey, mackerel, caranx, yellow jack, needlefish, conger, dorado, eel, turbot, grig, carp, etc.

Redfish. Sardine, tuna, mackerel, etc.

Fish in general, should be served in the same tray in which they are cooked. Some of the sauces in which fish may be served are: Tomato sauce, Tartar sauce, mayonnaise, vinegar sauce, gooseberry sauce, green sauce, etc.

Fried fish should be served immediately after frying. Grilled fish are served with oil, lemon, etc.

The fried fish must be dipped in flour and egg and fried in abundant hot oil. Fish must be seasoned carefully so that its own taste is not affected.

To counteract the poisoning from fish in bad conditions, strawberry, milk, and lemon, have excellent properties.

BACKED BREAM

Bream.—Oil.—Salt.—Parsley.—Lemon.—Onion.— Stock or water.—White wine.

When the bream is cleaned, make two or three cuts in the back of the fish and season with salt. In each cut, place a slice of lemon or onion. Sprinkle with hot oil and white and also with some big pieces of onion and a few branches of parsley. Place it in the oven and bake at 375° F for about 30 minutes. Serve it hot.

BACKED HAKE OR BREAM

One hake tail of about two pounds.—Three tbls. of butter.—One small cup of milk.—Bread crumbs.— Lemon.—Salt.—Pepper if desired.

Clean the fish and remove the skin. Season with salt and pepper and with lemon juice if desired. Put the fish. In an oven tray with milk and allow to stand for an hour and a half. Sprinkle then with grated cheese, chopped parsley and pieces of butter and bake again until it is cooked.

Slices of lemon are used as garnish.

BASS, VINEGAR SAUCE STYLE

Delicious fish, cooked the same as hake, angler, etc.
Cook it in boiling water with onion, wine, etc. Drain it
and add the vinegar sauce.

BOILED FISH

**Any kind of fish, specially white fish.—Lemon.—
Onion.—Garlic.—A squirt of white wine.—Salt.—
Celery if desired or laurel.—A squirt of oil.**

Place all the ingredients in enough cold water to cover
the fish but do not add the fish until the water is boiling.
Cook slowly for 10 minutes. Drain it carefuly and place it
on a tray.

It can be served with slices of lemon, sprinkled with
parsley, with «bechamel», mayonnaise, vinegar sauce,
white sauce, butter, etc.

BOILED HAKE

**Hake.—Onion.—Garlic.—Parsley.—Pimientos if
available.—White wine or sherry.—Oil.—Salt.—
Lemon.**

Clean the hake and put it in boiling water. Add a few
pieces of onion, parsley, garlic, a squirt of wine, pimientos
if available, a small slice of lemon, a squirt of oil, season
with salt and allow to cook for a few minutes.

The hake can be served with a small amount of the
liquid in which it was cooked or it can also be drained and
served with a sauce.

BREAM IN SAUCE

**Bream.—White wine.—Flour.—Butter.—Onion.—
Garlic.—Paprika.—Laurel.**

Clean the bream, season with salt, and fry in butter until it browns lightly. Remove the bream from the frying pan and place it in a casserole.

In the same butter, fry onion, garlic and chopped parsley. When it is lightly brown add a tbls. of flour and laurel, stock or water and a squirt of white wine. Season with salt, sieve it and pour this sauce on the bream. **Allow** it to cook for a few minutes with the sauce.

CODFISH «A LA BILBAÍNA»

One pound of codfish.—One chili pepper.—Butter.—Oil.—Onions.—Garlic.—A piece of ham.—Two hard boiled eggs.—Sugar.

If the codfish to be used is salted, cut it in pieces and place them in water for 10 hours with the chili pepper.

In one tbls. of butter and two tbls. of oil, fry one onion and a piece of ham all well chopped. When it is lightly brown, add a small cup of water and a chopped chili pepper. Pass this mixture through the sieve and add the two yolks from the hard boiled eggs and a tsp. of sugar. Mix thoroughly. The codfish is cooked in water with onion and garlic. When it is almost cooked, remove the bones and add the sauce to it. Let it cook with the sauce for a few minutes. Then it is ready to serve.

CODFISH «AMPARO»

Codfish.—Milk.—Flour.—Oil.—Onion.—Garlic.—Parsley.—Cinamon.

Cut the codfish into pieces and put them in water for 10 or 12 hours. Drain the water and place the codfish pieces in a deep tray and pour boiling milk over until it covers them. Let it stand for half an hour. After this time, drain the milk and dry the pieces with a cloth. Dip them in flour and fry them in hot oil. When the codfish pieces are fried, place them in a casserole. Make a sauce by frying onion, garlic and parsley all well chopped in oil and pour it over the codfish. After a few minutes, add the milk in which the codfish was previously soaked with a pinch of cinamon and allow to cook slowly until tender.

CODFISH WITH POTATOES

One pound of codfish.—Onion.—Potatoes.—Oil.— White wine.

Cut the codfish into pieces and soak them in water for 10 to 12 hours to desalt them. In an earthenware casserole place layers of chopped onion, codfish and slices of peeled potato. Add a good squirt of white wine, oil and enough water to cook. The layers will be in the order previously established trying to leave an onion layer on top. Put it in the oven. When the potatoes are cooked, remove it from the oven and serve in the same casserole.

CONGER IN GREEN SAUCE

Conger.—Flour.—Salt.—«Green sauce».

Cut the conger into slices, season with salt, dip them in flour and fry them in hot refined oil. Then place them in a casserole and pour the «green sauce» on top, allowing to cook. Serve with the sauce.

FISH PIES

From 14 to 16 pies.

One half pound of boiled fish chopped.—Three tbls. of butter or oil.—Seven to eight tbls. of a good flour.— Two tbls. of finely chopped onion.—Milk.—Bread crumbs.—Two branches of parsley.—Lemon.

Melt the butter in a casserole, add the onion and parsley and fry lightly stirring gently. Then add the flour, a squirt of lemon and the milk necessary to make a thick cream, stirring continously. Season with salt. Now add the chopped fish and allow to cook for 10 or 12 minutes. With a spoon take tbls. of the mixture, dip them in bread crumbs and fry them in hot oil. Drain them and serve them by themselves or accompanied by a sauce.

«CALDERETA»

Servings: 4

> **Two pounds of fish or shellfish.—For this dish you can use any combination of fish and shellfish you like, such as shrimps, mussels, clams, flounder, snapper, etc.—Two ripe tomatoes, seeded and chopped.— One large chopped onion.—One quarter cup of oil. Three branches of chopped parsley.—Two cloves of chopped garlic.—About one cup of water.—One cup of sherry or white wine.—One slice of bread.—Salt to taste.**

First the onion is fried lightly in a pot containing oil, until it is transparent. Next the rest of the vegetables are added and then the wine and water and the bread broken up. The washed seafood is placed nicely on top. The pot is covered and everything is brought to a boil for ten minutes. Season to taste with salt and pepper and serve hot.

CODFISH BASQUE STYLE

Servings: 3

> **One pound of dried codfish.—A little flour.—Two tbls. of tomato sauce.—One half cup of stock or water. Six cloves of garlic, well mashed. One half cup of olive oil.**

The codfish is soaked overnight similar to the method described in the recipe «Codfish Pil-Pil Style» The codfish is then drained, skinned, and cut into cubes, about one inch. Dry these pieces with a towel. Preheat the oil in a frying pan and then fry the garlic until it is brown, being careful not to burn it. Remove the garlic and in the oil, fry the cubes of fish previously sprinkled with flour. Next the fish is placed in a casserole and to it you also add the garlic, tomato sauce and the water or stock. Simmer this for about twenty minutes and serve it hot.

CODFISH PIL-PIL STYLE

Servings: 4

Two and a half pounds of dried codfish.—One quarter cup of oil.—One chopped onion.—One half tsp. of pepper.—Three quarters of a cup of fish stock.— Five cloves of crushed garlic.

This dish must never be stirred. The sauce is made by only shaking the pan. The codfish is soaked overnight and the water should be changed in the morning. When you are ready to prepare the fish, the scales should be removed without breaking the skin as it is the skin that gives the sauce the good flavour. When the fish has been cut into pieces, dry it with a cloth in order to get all the water out of it.

The garlic is crushed in a mortar and fried in oil until it is well browned. This garlic is then thrown away and half of the oil in which it was fried is poured into a saucepan. In this oil the onion is fried until it is golden, the fish is added with the skin side down, season it with salt and pepper and add the fish stock. This is simmered for about ten minutes and instead of stirring it, you shake the pan often in order to make the sauce. Once the sauce starts to get thick, you slowly add the oil that was left in the frying pan, continuing shaking the saucepan. When the sauce is smooth and thick (this takes about fifteen minutes over low heat) the dish is ready. Serve it with boiled potatoes or with rice.

FLOUNDER «A LA MOLINERA»

Fillets of flounder.—Butter.—Lemon.

Fry the fillets in oil. Place them on a tray, smear some butter on top, sprinkle with a squirt of lemon and place them for a few moments in the oven. Serve them hot.

FLOUNDER «AU GRATIN»

One pound of flounder.—Bread crumbs.—Parsley.— Salt.—Grated cheese.—Oil or butter.—Lemon.

Clean the fish, remove the dark skin and season with salt. Place it on an earthenware tray, cover with grated cheese and bread crumbs, sprinkle with chopped parsley and a few pieces of butter and add a squirt of lemon juice and another of refined oil.

Place it in the oven for 15 to 20 minutes. If it dries too much a little water or stock may be added.

FLOUNDER «MEUNIERE»

Flounder.—Flour.—Lemon.—Butter.—Parsley.— Peas.—Asparagus.

Remove the skin from flounder, cut it into fillets and take the spine off, which should be saved for later use.

Cut the fillets in half, dip them in flour, fry them in butter, place them afterwards on an earthenware tray and insert them in the oven for a few moments.

The spine is dipped in flour and fried. On top of it place the fillets, trying to reconstruct the original fish.

In the butter in which you fried the fillets, add a squirt of lemon, a little bit of water and pour this mixture over the flounder. Sprinkle with chopped parsley. Garnish with asparagus, peas and slices of lemon and place the tray for a few seconds into the oven.

If the peas to be used are fresh, they must be cooked previously.

FRESH CODFISH

Codfish.—Onion.—Parsley.—Salt.—Garlic.—Lemon.

Clean the fish and place it in a casserole with enough water to cover the fish. Season with salt, onion, garlic and parsley mashed in the mortar and a squirt of lemon. Allow it to cook.

The sauce is served separately from the fish.

FRIED FISH

To fry the fish, they must be cut into fine slices. After the fish are cleaned and washed, season with salt and dip them in flour. If the fish belongs to the category of «White fish» (described in the beginning of the chapter) then you can dip them in egg after doing it in flour.

Serve with slices of lemon.

All the fried fish must be done with abundant oil. The oil itself must be hot because if not, the fish would cook instead of fry. To serve drain the oil well. When frying the fish they should be turned over only once.

HAKE «A LA BILBAÍNA»

Servings: 3

One pound of hake.—One half pound of asparagus, or a small can.—One can of peas, or fresh.—Flour.—Garlic.—Parsley.—Salt.—Oil.

In a well greased casserole place one clove of garlic and two or three branches of parsley, all well chopped. On top of this you place the fillets or pieces of hake previously seansoned with salt and dipped in flour. The asparagu and peas are placed over the fish (if using fresch vegetables they must be cooked first). Add water enough so that it will not burn and to prevent it from getting too dry.

This will have to be checked occasionally as the fish is cooking. The dish is served in individual casseroles that are preheated by placing them in hot water and drying them. The hake is placed in these individual casseroles along with its sauce.

HAKE «A LA CAZUELA»

Two pounds of sliced hake.—Asparagus.—Peas.—Lettuce.—Clams.—Paprika.—Onion.—Garlic.—Flour.—Parsley.—Canned pimientos or roasted.—Oil.—Salt.—Pepper if desired.

The slices of hake are seasoned with salt, dipped in flour and fried. In hot oil, add the onion, garlic and parsley, all well chopped, a tbls. of flour, a pinch of paprika, a pinch of pepper if desired, and a small amount of stock or water. Put this mixture through the sieve into a casserole. The fried hake slices are placed on top of the liquid and then in the oven for a few minutes. Remove the fish from the oven and allow it to cook on the fire for another 5 minutes. Without letting it cool, garnish with seasoned lettuce, clams with a squirt of lemon, peas, strips of pimientos and asparagus and place everything in the oven for two or three minutes. Serve hot.

HAKE GALICIAN STYLE

One half pound of hake and a regular potato per person.—Garlic.—Paprika.—Oil.—Onion.—Parsley. Salt.

Peel the potatoes, cut them into slices, season them with salt and fry them lightly in hot oil with a few cloves of garlic. Remove some of the oil. To the remaining oil and potatoes add a pinch of paprika and water to allow them to cook completely. When the potatoes are cooking, add the hake slices, season with salt and allow to cook until the potatoes are tender.

To serve, place the hake slices in the center of the tray and the potatoes around them. The sauce in which they were cooked is poured over the tray.

HAKE IN SAUCE

Boiled hake.—Any sauce you prefer.—Lemon.

The hake is boiled or fried, drained from the water or oil and sprinklend with lemon juice. Cover it with the sauce of your preference.

HAKE PUDDING

One pound of hake.—Salt.—Bread crumbs.—One egg.—«Tomato sauce» or «Mayonnaise sauce».

Clean the hake, remove the bones and the skin and break it into small pieces. Add a beaten egg, two or three tbls. of bread crumbs, four or five tbls. of «tomato sauce» and the necessary salt. Mix thoroughly.

Prepare a well greased mold, sprinkled with bread crumbs. Place the mixture in the mold, sprinklesome bread crumbs on top and put it in the oven at medium heat. To see if the pudding is done, test it by sticking a knitting needle in it. If the needle comes out clean, the pudding is done.

Invert the mold on a tray to remove the pudding and pour over it the «mayonnaise sauce».

Garnish with lettuce, beet slices or red peppers.

HAKE TWO SAUCE STYLE

Hake (whole).—«Vinegar sauce».—«Mayonnaise sauce».

The hake is cooked similar to the recipe «Boiled hake». Clean the skin and place the fish on a tray along with the ingredients in which it was cooked. Separately you serve two sauces, «Vinegar sauce» and «Mayonnaise sauce» (both recipes are found under Sauces and Garnishes). This way each person can choose the sauce they like best, and some people even like to mix the two sauces as they give a very good flavour together.

The hake is adorned with branches of parsley.

LAMPREY ASTURIAN STYLE

One lamprey.—White wine.—One tbls. of chocolate. Oil.—Onion.—Garlic.—Parsley.—Thick paper.

Wash the lamprey with hot water and make a few slits in the back. Remove the intestines, collect the blood that comes out and reserve the liver. Fry in oil, onion, a small clove of garlic and parsley, all of them well chopped. Add a cup of white wine, the blood which you reserved, the grated chocolate and the chopped liver. Pour the sauce over the lamprey, season it with salt, place a thick paper over the pot and then cover it with a lid.

Allow to simmer and you may add a few tbls. of water if there is not sufficient sauce.

The sauce should be passed throuh the sieve before the dish is served.

OCTOPUS GALICIAN STYLE

Two pounds of octopus.—Oil.—Laurel.—Two big potatoes.—Paprika.—Salt.—Chili pepper.

Wash the octopus very well rubbing as if you were washing it. With a metal mortar or any other instrument, beat the octopus to make it release the sand it has in the suckers. Put it in water again and continue rubbing, making sure it is completely clean.

Boil water with two laurel leaves in a pot. When the water is boiling, seize the octopus by one end and introduce it three or four times in the water. When the octopus arms start to coil, leave it completely in the boiling water and allow it to boil for 20 minutes if the octopus is small and longer if it is bigger.

The potatoes are peeled, cut into big pieces and added to the octopus to cook. Stir occasinally so that it cooks evenly. When the octopus is cooked add a handful of salt. The octopus cooks better with the potatoes than alone. When cooked, cut it into small pieces and place it in the center of a long tray. Put the cooked potatoes at one end and the sliced hard boiled eggs at the other.

In hot oil fry a chopped chili pepper if desired.

The octopus, potatoes and eggs are sprinkled with paprika and with the oil in which the chili pepper was fried, previously sieved.

PERCH

This fish may be prepared in many different ways, baked, grilled, boiled, with sauces, etc.

This fish is good all year around and it is finer than sturgeon.

PICKLED FISH

Two pounds of fish.—Oil.—Vinegar of the best quality.—Garlic.—Laurel.—Onion.—Flour.

Wash and clean the fish, season with salt, dip it in flour and fry it in lots of oil. After the fish has been fried, in the same oil fry 5 or 6 cloves of garlic and a big onion cut into 6 pieces.

Place the fish in an earthenware casserole and then pour the oil with the cloves of garlic and onion. Add two leaves of laurel and enough vinegar to cover the fish. Place the casserole on the fire and allow to boil for two minutes. Remove from fire, place a thick paper on top of the casserole and cover with a lid to obtain a tight fitting. It is also convenient to add a small amount of gelatin to the pot.

ROASTED SARDINES

As soon as the fish have been cought (they are the fattest in late spring and summer) place them on a hot plate or on a grill, whole and without removing head or intestines.

SARDINES «REBOZADAS»

Sardines.—Flour.—Egg.—Oil.—Salt.

Wash the sardines, removing the intestines and the spine carefully. Starting from the head, lift the spine pulling gently towards the tail being careful not to remove the tail. Once the sardines are opened season with salt, dip in flour and egg and fry them in abundant oil. Drain the oil well from the sardines after frying. Place the sardines on the serving tray. They may be accompanied by tomato salad, lettuce, etc.

SOLE OR FLOUNDER

These fish are cooked similar to hake.

The best type of sole, is the one with grey skin and this one is preferred to the one with black skin. To clean the sole, remove the dark skin, intestines, etc.

It can be cooked as fried fillets, in the oven, boiled, etc. It may be accompanied by sauces, oysters, prawns, etc.

SQUIDS IN THEIR OWN INK

Servings: 4

One pound of squids.—Three branches of chopped parsley.—One tbls. of flour.—One quarter cup of red wine.—One small chopped onion.—One clove of mashed garlic.—One quarter cup of oil.—Salt and pepper to taste.

The squids are cleaned thoroughly, removing the outside skin, the intestines and their eyes. Wash the squids under cold running water and cut off their heads and tentacles. Remove the ink sac, and save it for later use. The body is cut into rings and the tentacles are cut into pieces. Over low heat you brown the garlic and then add the squids letting them fry for about three minutes and turning them frequently. Spread the flour over the squids and add the wine, salt, pepper and parsley. The ink sacs should be disolved in a little water, drained and the liquid then added to the rest of the ingredients. The chopped onion is added next and the pot covered. Allow the squids to cook over low heat until they are tender. This will take from 10 to 30 minutes depending on the squids.

When the squids are cooked, place them on a tray and if the sauce is too thick add a little more red wine. The sauce is then sieved and poured over the squids. This dish can be served with boiled potatoes or rice.

STEWED BREAM

Bream.—Onion.—Oil.—Salt.—Paprika.

Clean the bream and cut it in half. Place it in a casserole, add a small cup of water, a good squirt of oil, a few pieces of onion, a pinch of paprika, salt to season and allow to cook with regular fire.

Serve without sieving the sauce.

STEWED EELS

Eels.—Onion.—Salt.—Oil.—Stock or water.—Paprika if desired.

Remove the skin from the eels with hot water and fry them lightly whole or in pieces. In the same oil, fry later on, onion and garlic very well chopped, add stock or water and a pinch of paprika. Pour this mixture over the eels and allow to cook until they are tender.

Other variations consist in cooking the eels in «Green sauce», «Tomato sauce», «Sauce for fish», etc.

STUFFED SQUIDS OR «CHIPIRONES»

Servings: 6

Two pounds of squides (small).—One chopped onion.— One egg.—One cup of bread crumbs soaked in milk.— Six branches of finely chopped parsley.—Salt and pepper to taste.

First clean the squids very thoroughly as described in the recipe «Squids in their own ink». The tentacles should be chopped very fine and then combined with the other ingredients. Each squid is filled with this mixture and to close them you could either sew them or hold them together with a toothpick. Fry these stuffed squids lightly in oil, remove them from the pan and save the oil for the sauce.

Sauce:

Four tbls. of olive oil.—One or two sliced carrots.— One glass of white wine (sherry may be used as well).— Five tbls. of «tomato sauce».—Three or four branches of chopped parsley.—One half tsp. of saffron.— One regular size onion chopped finely.—One clove of mashed garlic.

The garlic is browned in the oil you saved from the stuffing. The chopped onion is then added and browned as well, after which you add the remaining ingredients. All this is boiled for five minutes and then poured over the stuffed squids.

Cook over low heat for about three quarters of an hour or until the squids are tender.

This dish may be eaten with rice or boiled potatoes.

STUFFED TROUT

One half pound trout for each person.—Slices of salted ham, cut thin.—Flour.—Three cloves of garlic.—Oil.

Heat oil in a large skillet and add the garlic cloves whole, which you fry until they are browned. The garlic is then discarded and the oil is saved for later use.

The trout are cleaned thoroughly and the opening for stuffing should be made as small as possible. The thinly sliced ham is rolled and stuffed through the opening at the gills When this is done, the trout should be sprinkled with salt, dipped lightly in flour and then fried in the oil previously reserved. The oil must be sizzling hot and the trout fried in it until it is browned on both sides.

This dish should be served immediately after frying.

TROUT «A LA MONTAÑESA»

Trout.—Onion.—Pepper.—Laurel.—Flour.—White wine.—Oil.

Clean the trout and season with salt two or three hours before cooking. Cook the trout in a casserole with a small glass of white wine, a small amount of water, a few pieces of onion, two grains of pepper and a leaf of laurel. When they are cooked, let them cool and pass the sauce through the sieve.

Fry a tbls. of flour in oil, add the sauce and allow it to boil for two or three minutes. Pour the sauce over the trout and serve.

TROUT WITH BACON

Trout.—Bacon.—Salt.—Oil.

Wash the trout and remove the intestines without breaking the body. Season with salt, stuff them with bacon and fry them. Serve them hot.

TUNA

Before frying the tunafish, in order to make it more juicy, it is convenient to cook it in water seasoned with salt, lemon, onion, garlic and parsley.

When the water starts to boil, place the tuna into it. The water will stop boiling. When the water starts to boil again, remove the tuna and drain the water from it. Fry the tuna and accompany it with sauce. The «Tomato sauce» goes well with this dish.

TUNAFISH «EN ROLLO»

One pound of tuna without skin or bones.—Onion.— Garlic.—Parsley.—Nutmeg.—Two eggs.—Bread crumbs.—Oil.—Salt.—Flour.—A piece of «tocino».

Remove the skin and bones from the tunafish and chop it finely. Add three tbls. of chopped onion, a branch of parsley and half a clove of garlic, everything well chopped, and the «tocino» also cut into small pieces. Then add a pinch of pepper, the nutmeg, two beaten eggs and season with salt. Mix thoroughly and make a roll with the mixture. Take the roll, dip it in bread crumbs and brown it lightly in abundant hot oil. Then place the roll in a casserole.

Fry some chopped onion and a tbls. of flour in part of the oil in which the roll was fried. Add a small amount of water, season with salt and pour this sauce over the roll allowing it to cook until done. To test, place a knitting needle in the roll and if it comes out clean the roll is done. Allow it to cool and cut the roll into slices. The sauce is sieved, poured over the slices of tunafish and everything is placed in the oven for a moment to warm it up before serving.

Meats

It is well known that once an animal has been killed, the meat hardens and gets tougher but later on it softens again and gets tender and easier to digest. The meat proteins contain all the aminoacids necessary for our organism to produce its own proteins.

The most abundant mineral salts in meat are: potasium, calcium and magnesium phosphates, sodium chloride and iron. The nutritional value of the meat varies according to its cooking preparation.

If meat is cooked in cold water, approximately 40 % of its nutritional value is passed to the water which is then called stock. On the surface of the stock you can see the grease and albumin.

However if the meat is placed into boiling water from the beginning, this causes the superficial albumin in the meat to coagulate quickly, preventing other substances from escaping. When meat is cooked like this, the stock would be rather tasteless but the meat itself will be much juicier and nutritional.

Frying meat has a similar effect on the meat as when you cook meat in boiling water. Before frying, meat is often dipped in flour, egg or bread crumbs, to prevent the meat from losing its juices.

For practical purposes, it is interesting to know that if meat appears bloody and red in colour after cooking, it is because it has not been cooked over 56° C. Meat should be cooked at 70° C or over to obtain its characteristic brown colour.

When eating pork, you should be careful regarding the amount of raw meat you consume, since raw meats that have not been inspected can carry trichinosis. This desease is caused by a microscopic worm which has often been deathly to man.

Leavings. There are two types of leavings, one being the red leavings and the other white leavings. The red ones are: blood, head, tongue, heart, lungs, liver, spleen, and kidneys. The white ones are: brain, thymus, pancreas, testicles, intestines, snout, feet and tits.

The red leavings except the lungs are more nutritious than the muscular meat. The meats in mamals are also divided into two classes: red and white.

Red meats consist of beff, cow, sheep, pork, soar, deer, rabbit, hare, horse, etc.

White meats consist of veal, suckling lamb, kid, etc.

In fowl, red meats are: goose, duck, young pigeon, partridge, pheasant, etc.

In fowl, white meats are: hen, chicken, turkey, Guinea hen, etc.

Red meats are generally more nutritious but more difficult to digest.

USAGE OF MEATS

Surloin.—First class meat.

Special for «turnedos», fillets, frits, etc.

When surloin is roasted it shrinks considerably but it is the juiciest meat.

Leg.—First class meat.

The word «legs» is used when referring to the hind part of the animal and «shoulder blade» is used when referring to the front part.

The legs of the pig are called hams.

The following sauces may accompany cooked meats: «Green sauce», «Tomato sauce», or you can make sauces with parsley, mustard, radishes or peppers. The following sauces may accompany roasted meats: Its own juice thickened with flour, an orange sauce apple sauce, or other cooked sauces.

«CHANFAINA»

Beef lights or lamb lights (lungs, liver, heart, etc.).— Onion.—Garlic.—Parsley.—Spices if desired.—Oil. Potatoes.—Laurel.

Cut the lights into small pieces and fry them lightly in the frying pan. The heart and lungs should be fried separately from the rest and then allow them to cook for two hours since they are tougher.

When this is done, drain the oil from the lights and place them in a casserole (except heart and lungs).

In the same oil fry onion, garlic and parsley chopped. Add some peeled potatoes cut in regular pieces. When everything is slightly fried, it is poured over the lights together with a leaf of laurel or any other herb you like and the boiling water necessary to cook. Add now the heart and lungs so that they can absorb the flavour. Serve in a deep tray with the sauce but not too much.

CHOPS «AL BATIN»

Lamb chops, two or three per person.—Salt.—Garlic. Flour.—Oil.—Milk.—Yeast.—Sherry or white wine.

Remove the meat from the straight part of the rib bone, leaving the meat only in the vertebra end. Fry them lightly in oil, not too hot and then sprinkle them with sherry.

In a small amount of hot milk, dissolve one half tsp. of yeast, a pinch of salt and flour to make a thick cream. Dip the chop in the cream but not the straight rib bone and fry them in abundant hot oil. Place them on a tray and serve them. To garnish you may use French fries, etc.

COLD ROAST BEEF

Beef surloin.—Oil.—Salt.

Tie the meat with a clean and resistant string so that the meat gets firm and compact. Place it in a deep tray, casserole, etc. Squirt with oil and put it in the oven for 20 minutes under strong heat. After this time, remove from the oven and sprinkle with salt.

Allow to cool, remove the string and cut the meat into slices.

This dish may also be served hot with potatoes and vegetables as garnish.

«ESCALOPES»

«Escalopes» are the fillets cut from the chops. They are dipped in flour, egg and bread crumbs and fried.

FILLETS «EMPANADOS»

The fillets «empanados» are made similar to «escalopes». They are seasoned with salt and mashed garlic, dipped in flour, egg, and bread crumbs and fried. The fillets should be fried in abundant oil that is not too hot so that the meat will be cooked through and not burned.

GRILLED PORK LOIN

Loin.—Pork lard.—Lemon.—Parsley.—Salt.—Wild marjoram.—Garlic.—Very small amount of white pepper.

Clean the loin well and remove the fat leaving only the pure meat. All the ingredients except the lard are mashed in a mortar with a small amount of salt. With this rub the loin and also sprinkle it with a small amount of lemon juice if it has not already been added to the mixture. The loin is tied well and left for one day so that the flavour may be absorbed throughout. When this time has passed, smear the loin well with pork lard and place it on a grill in the oven. Cook the loin and do not touch it during the cooking process. Once it is cold, it may be sliced and placed on a tray garnished with fruit, fresh vegetables, etc.

GRILLED LAMB CHOPS

One good size lamb chop for each person.—One clove of garlic well minced.—Salt to taste.—One tsp. of red pepper.

The lamb chops are sprinkled with garlic, salt and pepper and left to stand with these ingredients for about 30 minutes. The chops are then fried on a hot grill.

HIGHLY SEASONED «CALLOS A LA MADRILEÑA»

Servings: 6

About two pounds of tripe.—One quarter cup of oil.— A couple of leeks.—Three quarters of a cup of white wine.—One and a half tsp. of salt.—Four slices of bacon.—One «chorizo».—One leaf of laurel.— Three tbls. of ketchup or «tomato sauce».—About two ounces of parsley well chopped.—Two cups of stock.—Three cloves of garlic.—Ten or twelve peppercorns.—Two onions, one diced and the other sliced.—Three quarters of a cup of sherry.—A foot from a calf.—Rock salt, three tbls.—Three regular size carrots.—Two tbls. of marjoram.—One normal size lemon.—Three tbls. of vinegar.

The tripe is cleaned by washing it well in severals sets of water. Rub the tripe with rock salt and lemon. Now place it in water containing vinegar, for about thirty minutes. This water is discarded and the tripe is boiled for fifteen minutes in anough fresh water to cover it and then drained.

Reserve the water for later use. The calf's foot is split lengthwise and placed in a sauce pan along with the tripe, sliced onion, cloves of garlic, chopped carrots, seasoning, parsley, wine, sherry and stock. All these ingredients are brought to boiling point and then left to cook over very low heat for three hours. When it has been cooked allow it to cool. Cut the tripe into square pieces and also remove the meat from the calf's foot and dice it. The bacon, «chorizo» and chopped onion are fried together in a pan containing the oil.

When this has fried for a few minutes, add the tripe, trotter, ketchup or «tomato sauce» and the peppercorns. All this is browned slowly and then transferred into an earthenware dish. The liquid left from the tripe is poured over everything and then simmered for another two hours.

KIDNEYS ASTURIAN STYLE

One kidney from a veal.—A small glass of cider.— A tsp. of brandy.—A tsp. of flour.—A tbls. of butter.— A small clove of garlic.—Salt.—Onion.—Oil.

Wash and clean the kidney, cut in into pieces, season with salt and fry them in half a tbls. of oil. Place them in a sieve and let them drain. Then fry them again in very hot butter with garlic and a big piece of onion. When the pieces of the kidney are lightly brown remove them from the pan and let them drain. Remove also the garlic and onion and add the flour to the butter. After a few moments add the cider and brandy if desired and let it cook for a brief time to thicken. Pour this sauce over the kidneys and serve hot (Be careful not to let the kidneys get cold).

KIDNEYS IN SHERRY

Kidneys.—Oil or butter.—Ham.—Onion.—Parsley. Sherry.—Pepper.—Tomato.—Salt.

Clean the kidneys, cut them into pieces and fry them in a tbls. of oil over strong heat. After this, drain them.

Fry a few dice of ham in butter or oil and add small amounts of onion, garlic and parsley finely chopped and half a small glass of sherry. Add now the kidneys, a pinch of pepper and two tbls. of tomato sauce and allow to cook for 5 minutes until there is no blood visible in the kidneys.

Serve them with sauce. They may be accompanied by white rice.

LARDED MEAT

Veal.—«Tocino».—Ham.—White wine.—Salt.—Oil. Butter.—Onion.—Laurel.—Garlic.—Spices if desired.—Tomatoes.

Lard the meat with «tocino» and ham. (This is the process of drilling a few holes through the meat and stuffing them with bacon, ham or «tocino»). Fry the meat lightly in oil. In the same oil fry chopped onion, garlic, a leaf of laurel and tomatoes without skin or seeds. You can add spices if you want. Pour this sauce over the meat together with a squirt of white wine and the necessary water to cook. Once the meat is cooked, remove it from the sauce and cut it into slices.

Serve together with with the sieved sauce. Garnish with potato puffs.

LIVER «EMPANADO»

Liver.—Bread crumbs.—Salt.—Oil.—Egg.

Season the liver with salt, dip it in bread crumbs, then in egg and fry it in oil but not too hot. Drain the oil well and place it on a tray to serve immediately. To cook this dish the liver must be cut into fillets.

LOIN IN MILK

One pound of loin.—Milk.—Salt.—Garlic.

Season the loin with salt and mashed garlic and place it in a casserole covered with milk. Allow to stand for an hour; after this time let it cook in the same milk turning it once in a while until it gets lightly brown.

The loin is cut into slices and served with the remaining milk once this has been sieved.

Garnish with French fries, mashed vegetables, etc.

MEAT BALLS

One half pound of ground pork meat.—One pound of ground veal.—Three ounces of lard.—Two tbls. of flour.—One cup of oil.—Two tbls. of finely chopped parsley.—Three small cloves of garlic mashed in a mortar.—Two eggs.—Two slices of bread soaked in milk.—One clove.—One cup of water.—One quarter cup of white wine.—Two tbls. of ketchup or tomato sauce.—Two tbls. of flour.—One regular size onion, well diced.—Two small carrots, chopped.—Salt and pepper to taste.

Sauce.—First the lard is heated in a frying pan, after which the carrots and onion are added and allowed to fry for four minutes. Two tbls. of flour are added next and when this is light brown, add the ketchup or tomato sauce, water, salt, wine, clove and pepper.

When these ingredients are boiling, you should skim the foam off which forms. Turn the heat down, and allow the sauce to simmer for a good hour. Stir the sauce occasionally so that it will not stick.

Meat balls.—The bread that has been soaked in milk is mashed very thoroughly. The bread, veal, pork, parsley, garlic, eggs, salt and pepper are all mixed together and stirred until all the ingredients are well blended. To form the meat balls you can put about a tbls. of flour in a glass and placing a good tsp. of the meat paste in it, shake the covered glass until the meat forms a ball. More flour is added when needed and this procedure is continued until all the meat paste has been used. As the meat balls are formed, they are placed on a plate which also contains a light layer of flour.

To fry the meat balls, place them in oil which has been preheated and fry them until they are well browned.

The previously prepared sauce is sieved to remove any lumps and then poured over the meat balls. Over very slow heat, allow it to cook for about half an hour and if the sauce should be thick, you may add a little boiling water. This recipe should give you approximately three dozen meat balls.

MEAT «CANUTOS»

One pound of fillets.—A piece of ham.—Leavings from fowl.—Onion.—Garlic.—Parsley.—Oil or butter.—Salt.—Flour.

Trim the fillets to equal them in size, spread them with chopped ham, the fowl leavings and the trimmed pieces of meat, season with salt, add also a small amount of onion, garlic and parsley chopped. Roll the fillets and tie them with a string. Fry them lightly.

Prepare a sauce by frying in oil or butter a small amount of onion and flour. Cook the rolls in this sauce. Once they are cooked, remove the strings and serve them with the sauce previously passed through the sieve.

MEAT JUICE

Lean meat.—Salt.

Make several slits to the meat in one direction and then perpendicularly on both sides. Add a very small amount of salt. Place the meat in a small container so that it is not too loose. Cover the container tightly and place it in a double boiler for half an hour. Collect the juice from the meat. It is a good reconstituent.

MEAT ROLL

One pound of chopped meat.—One half pound of chopped liver.—Eggs.—Bread crumbs.—«Tocino».— Ham.—Onion.—Garlic.—Parsley.—Oil.—Salt.

Season the meat and chopped liver with mashed salt, garlic and parsley, one half small onion well chopped, two beaten eggs, a piece of ham and another of «tocino» both well chopped. You may add spices if you wish. Taste for salt and add four tbls. of bread crumbs. Form the meat into a roll and stuff both ends of the roll with a whole hard boiled egg so that the eggs are covered by the meat as well. Fry the roll in abundant hot oil until evenly brown and then place it on a tray containing pieces of onion and a few tbls. of stock. Insert the tray in the oven until the meat is cooked throughout. The meat roll may be covered with slices of «tocino» to prevent it from burning.

Let it cool, cut it into slices and serve them with «tomato sauce» or any other.

«MORCILLO» IN ITS JUICE

One pound of meat from the leg of a cow.—Oil.— Onion.—Salt.—White wine.

Clean the meat by removing the nerves and cook these in a small amount of cold water. In a little bit of oil, fry a tbls. of chopped onion. The oil, onion and a tbls. of white wine are added to the water in which the nerves were cooked. (The nerves are discarded). The meat is placed with this mixture, everything is seasoned with salt and allowed to cook until the meat is tender.

Serve the «morcillo» in its juice garnished with peas, artichokes, carrots, etc.

ROAST BEEF

Loin.—Pork lard.—Onion.—Salt.—Oil.—Thick paper.

Clean the loin well removing nerves and fat.

Tie the meat firmly in a good shape, season it with salt and sprinkle it with oil and pork lard. Cover it with a greased thick paper, place it in an oven pan containing chopped onion and whatever pieces of meat you may have trimmed off the loin. Next, place it in the oven under strong heat and if you think there is not enough juice to keep it from burning, you may add some tbls. of white wine or water. When the meat is done, (some people prefer roast beef to be rather red and raw in the center) place it in a covered casserole and leave it near the fire or in the warm oven to keep it warm until it is ready to be served.

The juice and the onion left in the oven pan should be heated up with a bit of water, allowed to boil for a few minutes, sieved and this then serves as the sauce for the roast beef.

The roast beef is sliced, placed on a tray and served with its sauce.

The tray may be adorned with lettuce, carrots, French fries, etc.

ROASTED LAMB

Two pounds of lamb.—Onion.—Garlic.—Parsley.—Oil.—Pepper grains.—Laurel.—Thyme.—White wine.—Salt.

Season the lamb with salt, mashed garlic, parsley and pepper. Place it on an earthenware tray, drench it with white wine and oil and around the meat put a few leaves of thyme and laurel. Cover the lamb with rings of onion and leave it in the oven to roast. On top of it, place a piece of heavily greased paper so that it will not burn. Before serving, the sauce should be sieved.

ROASTED LAMB ENGLISH STYLE

One leg of lamb.—Salt.—«Mayonnaise».

Clean the leg, removing nerves and fat. Next, tie it so that it will not lose its shape and place it to cook in boiling water together with whatever pieces of meat you may have trimmed off the leg. When the leg is cooked, remove the string and cover the leg with a coat of wet rock salt. Place the leg on a grill under which you will have put a tray with water. The meat must not touch the water. Place everything in the oven under strong heat until the leg is tender. Remove the excess of salt.

To serve, accompany this dish with a «Mayonnaise sauce» (the recipe for this sauce is given in the chapter of Sauces and Garnishes).

ROASTED LEG OF LAMB

One leg of lamb weighing from four to five pounds.— One half tsp. of dried thyme.—One quarter cup of cognac.—Three tbls. of olive oil.—One half dozen whole black pepper grains.—About one half cup of water.—One good size bunch of parsley, well chopped. Three cloves of garlic mashed in a mortar.—One regular onion chopped very finely.

The oven should be preheated to about 400° F. Excess fat and thick skin is trimmed from the leg of lamb. The leg is then rubbed with salt and browned in an earthenware casserole containing two tbls. of olive oil. The browning will take at least twenty minutes. When this is done, the leg is placed on a roasting pan in the oven with the fat side up. To prevent the meat from burning, add one quarter cup of water and use this and the meat juice which is formed to baste the leg (more water will have to be added as the leg of lamb roasts, to keep it moist).

The grease from the casserole in which the lamb was browned can be discarded. Heat a tbls. of fresh olive oil and in this fry the chopped onion, mashed garlic, parsley, dried

121

thyme and whole pepper grains, until the onion and garlic are soft.

When the roast is half done, pour the cognac over it and spread the onion and herb mixture on top of it as well. Continue to baste the lamb until done. (This size leg of lamb will take approximately two hours to cook through). When cooked, the lamb should be firm enough that it can be carved. The lamb is served with the sauce.

ROASTED SUCKLING PIG

One pig, not older than 21 days.—The pig should weigh about six and a half pounds once it has been cleaned and dressed.—Five cloves of chopped garlic.—Two diced onions, normal size.—One bunch of parsley, chopped.—One half tsp. of powered thyme.—A leaf of laurel.—Half a cup of water.—Half a cup of white wine, a dry wine is recomended.—One half pound of lard.—Salt.—Pepper.

The pig is slit open from head to tail and stuffed with the thyme, laurel, garlic, onions, and parsley. Sprinkle the pig with salt and pepper and place it in an earthenware dish. Add water and wine until the bottom of the dish is covered. You should need about one half cup of each. The lard is added and the pig is placed in a preheated oven at a moderate temperature for one hour. When this time is up, turn the pig over and if there is a lot of juice, you may pour some of it off. Rubb the pig with oil or lard and continue roasting it until the meat is tender and the skin is crusty and golden brown. While roasting, the pig should be basted frecuently.

ROLLED MEAT

One pound fillet.—One half pound of lean meat or sausages.—«Tocino».—Red peppers.—Onion.—Garlic.—Parsley.—Salt.—Oil.—One egg.—Bread crumbs.

Season the meat with salt mashed garlic and parsley.

Pound the meat. If the red peppers are not canned, they must be roasted and cut into strips. Cut also the lean meat and «tocino» in strips. On the pounded fillet place alternate strips of meat and «tocino».

Beat the egg and mix it with a tbls. of bread crumbs. This mixture is poured over the meat and this is then rolled and tied firmly. Fry the roll lightly in hot oil, smear some butter on it, put a few strips of «tocino» on top, pour over it a squirt of white wine, put a few pieces of onion on the same tray and allow to bake in the oven. All these ingredients must be covered by a well greased paper to prevent them from burning.

The sauce is sieved and served hot with the roll of meat from which you have previously removed the string used to tie the roll up.

RUSSIAN FILLETS

Chopped meat.—Oil.—Salt.—Garlic.—Milk.—Flour. Egg.

The chopped meat is seasoned with salt and mashed garlic. Mix some flour in a small amount of milk and pour this mixture over the meat blending the ingredients thoroughly. From this paste take a tablespoonful and fry it until lightly brown on one side. Turn it over and flatten it with a skimmer. Drain the oil from the fillets and serve them on a tray immediately.

SAUSAGES

Place the raw sausages in a pot over low heat so that they will cook slowly in the juice that they themselves release. A small amount of water may be added. Sausages can be prepared boiled, fried, roasted, etc.

SIRLOIN

The two best ways to prepare sirloin is to fry it on a hot plate or in the oven.

Pork meat and also veal and beef acquire an excelent taste when they are seasoned with salt and mashed garlic, especially if they are going to be fried.

STEAKS «ENCEBOLLADOS»

Beefsteak or fillets.—Onion.—Garlic.—Parsley.— Oil.—Salt.—White wine.

Chop a good amount of onion with a small amount of garlic and a few branches of parsley and season this with salt. The fillets or steaks are also seasoned with salt.

In a casserole or a pressure cooker place a layer of the onion mixture, next a layer of fillets, again onion and continue this process ending with a layer of onion. When this is done, add a squirt of white wine and a small squirt of oil. Cover with a tight fitting lid and allow it to cook over low heat until the meat is tender.

STEWED LAMB WITH POTATOES

Servings: 6

Two pounds of tender lamb.—Two cloves of garlic, chopped.—Half a dozen branches of chopped parsley. A squirt of vinegar.—One pound of small new potatoes.—One quarter cup of oil.—Salt and pepper to taste.—One onion sliced.—A bit of paprika.—A small amount of white wine may be added if desired.

The lamb is cut into good size cubes and these are slightly prefried in oil before the other ingredients are added. Add all the remaining ingredients and a small amount of water so that the stew will not burn. Cover the pan and allow the stew to simmer until the meat and potatoes are tender. The cooking time will be around twenty-five minutes. Taste stew for salt.

124

STEWED SWEETBREADS AND OTHERS

Sweetbreads.—«Tocino».—Leeks or onions.—Garlic. Parsley.—Salt.—White wine.—Stock or water.

Clean the sweetbreads thoroughly and wash them afterwards. Soak them for an hour in stock or cold water. After this time place them in boiling water with onion, garlic, parsley, leeks, etc., a squirt of white wine and season with salt. Cook until they are tender.

There are many other ways to prepare sweetbreads. One variation is to cook them like before. After five minutes of boiling, skim the foam off, remove them form the water and discard the skin of the sweetbreads. Dry them with a cloth, cut them into small pieces and fry them. You may garnish this dish with vegetables, peas, carrots, etc.

STEWED VEAL

One pound of veal from the leg.—Two tbls. of lard or oil.—Garlic.—Tender carrots.—Tomato.—Onion. Salt.—White wine.

In the oil or lard, fry the meat seasoned with salt until lightly brown, together with a few whole cloves of garlic. Add then a regular peeled carrot and a few big pieces of onion. After a few moments add a glass of white wine and allow to simmer for half an hour.

Once the meat is cooked, allow it to cool and cut it into slices. Add a small amount of water to the sauce, boil momentarily and pass it through the sieve. Pour the sauce over the meat and serve. Garnish with vegetables, mashed potatoes, etc.

STEWED VEAL WITH MACARONI

One pound and a half of veal.—One half pound of macaroni.—One tbls. of grated cheese.—One half onion.—One bulb of garlic, clean but without peel-

ing.—A small leaf of laurel.—Oil.—A small glass of white wine.—A small glass of stock or water.—One half lemon.—Salt.

Season the veal with salt, cut it into pieces and cook it with all the ingredients except macaroni and cheese.

Cook the macaroni with a lot of boiling water seasoned with salt. When they are almost done, drain the water from them and add them to the veal (at this point, the veal must be almost cooked too) together with the cheese. The cheese may be eliminated if desired. Finish cooking and rectify the salt if necessary. Serve garnished with pieces of fried bread.

TONGUE

Tongue may be prepared in many different ways but first of all it must be washed well and peeled. To peel the tongue, hold it by the base and dip it in and out of boiling water repeatedly. If after this it is not possible to remove the skin, you can cook the tongue along with the other ingredients and use the water to make the sauce for that particular dish. After this cooking time, the tongue would be easily peeled.

TONGUE «REBOZADA»

The tongue is cleaned and peeled as described under «Tongue». Cook the tongue in stock seasoned with salt, adding a bit of onion, parsley, garlic, carrots and a few leaves of laurel. When the tongue is cooked through and tender, it can now be peeled if you were not able to peel it previously.

Cut the tongue into fillets, dip them in flour, egg and bread crumbs. Fry them and then allow them to cook in the stock in which the tongue was boiled. This stock should be passed through the sieve first.

126

Fowl and game

CANNED PARTRIDGES

**Partridges.—Oil.—Garlic.—Pepper.—Salt.—
Laurel.—Vinegar or lemon juice.**

Clean the partridges and soak them in cold water for four hours. During these four hours the water should be changed frequently so that the partridges will be thoroughly clean and the meat white. The partridges should then be removed and dried with a cloth. Season them with salt, garlic and pepper. Fry them in abundant oil and then place them in earthenware casseroles. Per partridge, fry three cloves of garlic, a leaf of laurel, a tbls. of lemon juice or vinegar and pour this over the partridges. Cover the partridges with oil and cook them. Once they are cook and tender, let them cool and place them in conserving jars or in the earthenware casseroles, well covered with oil and tightly closed.

If they are kept in a cool place, they can be preserved up to three months.

CHICKEN «AL AJILLO»

A chicken.—Salt.—Half a dozen cloves of garlic.—Oil.—Grease or lard.

Clean the chicken well and whole or cut into serving pieces season it with salt, smear it with grease or lard or sprinkle it with refined oil. Next sprinkle it with chopped garlic. Place it in the oven until it is tender and serve it very hot.

CHICKEN «A LA CAZUELA»

One two pound chicken.—Six or eight salad onions.—Dry sherry.—Oil.—One large carrot.—A small can of mushrooms.

The day before, clean and season the chicken. The chicken may be seasoned with a mixture of salt, mashed garlic, pepper, parsley and other spices if desired.

The next day, bfown the chicken whole or in pieces by frying it in oil. Remove it from the frying pan and place it in a casserole. In the same oil in which you fried the chicken, now fry the salad onions slightly chopped, the carrot cut into slices and the mushrooms cut in halves. Add a good squirt of sherry or a dry white wine. Pour this mixture over the chicken, cover the casserole tightly and cook this over moderate heat. When the chicken is tender, serve it adorned with its sauce.

CHICKEN «AL CHILINDRON»

Chicken.—Oil.—Tomato.—Onion.—Peppers.—Ham.

Once the chicken or chickens have been cleaned, parted and seasoned as usual, fry them in hot oil. Next add a small amount of chopped onion, pieces of ham, pieces of peppers, a tomato without the peel or seeds, until the chickens are covered. Allow this to cook over low heat without adding water.

By cooking, the sauce will reduce itself.

CHICKEN «EN PEPITORIA»

One chicken cut into pieces.—One regular onion
chopped finely.—Two cloves of mashed garlic.—
One chicken liver.—Two hard boiled egg yolks.—
Oil.—Two slices of bread without the crust.—Two
branches of parsley.—One slice of smoked ham.—
One third of a cup of sherry.—Two ounces of peeled
almonds.—Half a dozen peppercorns.—Three quarters
of a cup of white wine.—One half cup of stock.

The chicken is cut into pieces and fried in oil until it is
golden brown.

The chicken is removed and the same oil is used to fry
the chopped onion.

Put the chicken into a saucepan and cover it with stock
and water. The onion is then added as well as the oil in
which it was fried. When this has simmered for thirty minutes, add the wine and peppercorns.

The chicken liver, almonds, garlic, and bread are fried
separately and when they are done, they are placed in the
mortar along with the parsley and egg yolks. These ingredients are then mashed until they form a paste. Add the
sherry, stir well and pour this mixture over the chicken.
Allow the chicken to simmer for another twenty minutes.
Taste the sauce which forms for salt and if the sauce should
be too thin when the chicken is done, remove the chicken,
boil the sauce down and then reheat the chicken when it
is ready to serve.

This dish may be served with French fries.

CHICKEN IN BRANDY

One tender chicken.—One piece of dried ham.—
Four tbls. of pork lard or oil.—Stock or water.—
Brandy.—Onion.—Salt.—Oil.

Clean the chicken and in the center sprinkle it with
salt and stuff it with a small onion and a piece of ham. Bind
it with a string and spread the chicken with lard.

Fry some pieces of ham in a small amount of oil. Remove the ham and pour the oil in the same pot as the chicken. Cover the pot with a heavy piece of paper and then the lid so that it will be tightly closed. Place it in the oven under moderate heat. Turn the chicken over occasionally and when it is golden brown add a few pieces of onion, a squirt of brandy and then cover it again allowing to cook this time under low heat.

Add a small amount of stock or water to the juice from the chicken and bring it to a boil. This sauce is then separated and used to serve with the chicken. This dish may be garnished with fried onions previously cooked, potatoes, etc. Serve hot.

CHICKEN STUFFED WITH TRUFFLES

This dish is made similarly to the recipe for. «Hen stuffed with truffles».

DUCK WITH ASPARAGUS

One duck.—One half pound of chopped meat.—One quarter of a pound of ham.—A half pound of lean pork meat.—Pork lard.—Lemon.—Onion.—Garlic. Parsley.—Dry sherry.—Asparagus.

Clean the duck, season the inside with salt and smear it with pork lard and lemon. Stuff the duck with the chopped meat, lean pork meat also chopped and the ham cut into small pieces. To these meats previously add a chopped branch of parsley, a clove of garlic, spices if desired and the necessary salt. Once the duck is stuffed, sew it together and tie it. Smear the outside of the duck with pork lard and pour a small cup of dry sherry over it. The duck must have been previously placed in a casserole. After adding the sherry, pour also a small cup of water in the casserole After adding the sherry, pour also a small cup of water and insert it into the oven. When it is done, serve it with the sauce and garnished with asparagus.

DUCK WITH TURNIPS

One duck.—Four slices of bacon.—Four regular sliced
carrots.—One glass of white wine.—One cup of
stock.—A pinch of ginger.—Salt and pepper to taste.
One pound of turnips.—Three tbls. of lard.

When the duck has been well cleaned, wrap the slices
of bacon around it and place it in a pan with a tbls. of lard.
The duck should be browned lightly and then allowed to
cook for about an hour until it is tender. The stock, wine,
ginger, carrots and seasonings are then added.

Clean the turnips well (they may have to be cut through
if they are really fat) and fry them until they are browned
evenly in a tbls. of lard. They are then placed in boiling
water and should cook for five minutes. When the turnips are cooked, they are added to the duck to absorb
flavour from the juice. When ready to serve, place the duck
on a tray surrounded by the turnips and other vegetables
if desired.

HARE PIE

One hare.—Salt.—Garlic.—Sherry.—Bread crumbs.
A small can of truffles.—«Tocino».—Ham.—Brandy.
One half pound of chopped veal.—One half pound of
lean pork meat.—Two eggs.—«Hojaldre».

Clean hare, cut it into pieces, season it with salt and
garlic and leave it outside for one or two days. Clean the
meat from the bones and cut it into strips. Combine these
strips of meat with strips of «tocino», ham and the truffles.
Sprinkle these meats with brandy.

The chopped veal and pork are mixed with one quarter
of a cup of sherry, two well beaten eggs and one tbls. of
bread crumbs. Line a mold with the «hojaldre» dough.
Fill the mold with alternate layers of chopped meat, strips
of hare, strips of «tocino» and ham and the chopped
truffles. Cover the mold with a layer of dough and put it
in the oven. Cover the pie with a greased sheet of paper

so that the meat will cook through without burning the dough. To test the pie to see if it is done, pinch it with a knitting needle.

HARE WITH BROAD BEANS

One hare.—Oil.—Onion.—Garlic.—Parsley.—Mint or any other aromatic herb.—Broad beans.—Salt.—Laurel.—Ham.—A knee bone from a cow.—One half pound of beef.

Once the hare has been cleaned, season it with salt, garlic and parsley, all of these mashed in a mortar. Leave the hare with this seasoning for no less than one night. The beans should be soaked overnight in water as well.

The next day, prepare a stock with a small amount of water, a piece of onion, a clove of garlic, a few branches of parsley, a leaf of laurel, the bone, the beef, a piece of ham and mint or other aromatic herbsif you like.

The broad beans are placed to cook in a small amount of boiling water seasoned with garlic, onion, parsley and laurel. Do not add salt. Let them boil until they are almost tender.

The hare is cut into pieces, fried and then cooked in the stock previously prepared. When the hare is almost cooked, add the broad beans and let them finish cooking together seasoning with salt. There should only be enough liquid to prevent it from burning.

To serve remove the bone, beef, ham, garlic, laurel, etc. so that you only have the beans and hare remaining.

This dish is served hot and may be accompanied by a salad.

HEN STUFFED WITH TRUFFLES

One hen.—Veal meat, ham, etc. for the stuffing all chopped.—Stock to cook the hen (onion, garlic, parsley, beef bone, calf hoof, a piece of ham, one carrot, etc.).—A small can of truffles.—Salt and other spices if desired.—Sherry or white wine.

Clean the chicken and singe well over the stove. Cut the hen at the first wing joint and discard the tips. Disjoint the bones in the upper part of the wings and by massaging the wings outwards, this bone can be removed. Remove the neck and sew the opening together.

Make a slit along the spine separating the meat from the vertebras and the ribs. Through this opening, remove the bones from the legs, breast, etc.

When this is done, remove the intestines, etc.

The hen is stuffed through this opening. Make a stuffing with salt, spices if desired, chopped truffles, the meats and ham chopped, a quarter of a cup of sherry and mix everything well. When the hen has been stuffed, sew it together and place it to cook in a stock made the following way: Place a few pieces of onion, a clove of garlic, a few branches of parsley, a knee bone from a cow, a calf hoof, a piece of ham, a carrot, the giblets from the hen, etc. in cold water. When the stock has boiled for an hour, add the hen and allow to cook. When the hen is cooked, let it cool and serve it sliced. The sauce is served separately.

JACKSNIPE

After the jacksnipes have been cleaned and seasoned, they are left outside for two days. Jacksnipes can be prepared similar to other recipes for game i.e. stewed, roasted, etc.

PARTRIDGES «A LA MONTAÑESA»

Partridge.—Onion.—Paprika.—Parsley.—Oil.— Salt.—Lemon.

Clean and season the partridge and leave it outside for two days. After this time, cut the partridge into pieces and fry them in oil until they are golden brown. In a small amount of oil, fry a few pieces of onion, chopped parsley, paprika and a squirt of lemon. This mixture is poured over the partridge and it is then cooked with only enough liquid to prevent it from burning.

PARTRIDGES WITH CABBAGE

Three partridges, young and tender.—Two cloves of whole peeled garlic.—One regular onion.—One third cup of olive oil.—Flour.—One egg well beaten.— One large head of cabbage.—One half of a leaf of laurel.—A pinch of powdered cinnamon.—One cup of stock or beef bouillon.—Half a cup of white wine, a dry wine is recomended.—One regular size tomato.— Salt and pepper to taste.

The partridges should be washed and dried well. In a slightly greased oven pan containing the whole onion, garlic and tomato, place the partridges rubbed with oil and sprinkled with salt and pepper. The pan is placed in a preheated oven. When the partridges are half done (this will take about twenty minutes), add the white wine and when this wine has nearly evaporated add the stock, laurel and cinnamon. The partridges should be basted frecuently so it may be necessary to add more stock in order to maintain an abundant amount of liquid.

During the cooking process of the partridges, prepare the cabbage. The cabbage leaves are separated and boiled whole in salted water until they are tender but not too soft. They are then drained and rinsed in cold water. Form the cabbage into rolls by placing three leaves on top of each other and rolling them. The cabbage may be held in place either with a toothpick or tied with a string. Each roll is then sprinkled with flour, dipped in egg and fried in oil until they are browned on all sides.

The cabbage should be added to the partridges a quarter of an hour before the partridges are cooked to absorb the flavour of the sauce.

To serve, the sauce is sieved and poured over the partridges which should be cut in two. The cabbage is placed around the partridges on the serving tray.

QUAIL

Quail is cooked similar to chicken.

134

QUAILS IN NESTS

Quails.—A piece of «Tocino» from the ham.—Onion. Garlic.—Salt.—Parsley.—Potatoes.—Eggs.—Flour.

Pluck the quails and clean them without wetting them or cutting their heads off. Remove eyes and legs and wash the bill well to remove any dirt that could be present. The quails are seasoned with salt, garlic and parsley mashed in a mortar and the wings and legs are tied to the body.

Chop a little bit of onion and place it on a refractory tray. On top of the onion place the quail or quails sprinkled with oil and covered with slices of «tocino». Insert them into the oven.

Peel the potatoes and cut them really thin like straws. Fry them in oil and season them with salt. Beat an egg, mix it with a tsp. of flour and pour it over the fried potatoes.

In a casserole or small tray, make a nest with the mixture of potatoes and egg and place these nests momentarily in the oven until the egg sets.

Remove them from the oven and place a quail in each nest after they have been done. Previously you must have removed the slices of «tocino» and cut the string around the quails. The juice from the quails is served separately.

RABBIT «EN ADOBO»

Rabbits.— Onions. —Garlic.—Laurel.—Paprika.— Lemon.—Parsley.

Clean the rabbits and season them with salt, mashed garlic and parsley, chopped onion, paprika and the juice of a small lemon. Allow to stand with this mixture for about 13 hours. In the same casserole in which they have been seasoned, they are cooked by adding oil first and later on the stock or water to finish cooking. The casserole must have a tight fitting lid and the rabbits should not be stirred (shake the casserole gently occasionally). Serve them with their own sauce.

135

RABBIT IN BRANDY

Rabbit.—Brandy.—Pepper.—Onion.—Stock or water.—Butter.—Oil.

Clean the rabbit and leave it overnight with the seasoning consisting of salt, mashed garlic and parsley and some aromatic herb. Cut the rabbit into pieces and fry them in butter and oil adding a small amount of chopped onion, a small cup of brandy and a pinch of pepper if desired. Add also some stock or water and allow to cook.

To serve, the sauce is passed through the sieve and poured over the meat. If the sauce is too thin, you can thicken it by adding some hard boiled egg yolks.

RABBIT WITH SALAD

Rabbit.—Butter.—Peas.—Onion.—Garlic.—Salt.— Parsley.—Other herbs.—Laurl.—One half pound of veal.—One bone.—A piece of ham.

Clean the rabbit, season it with salt, mashed garlic and parsley, mint, etc. and leave it with these ingredients over night. Cut the rabbit in rather small pieces and fry them in butter. In the same butter, fry later on a small chopped onion, peas, a branch of parsley and a leaf of laurel.

With the meat and bone, make a stock and pour it over the rabbit pieces together with the onion, peas, etc.

Allow to cook until tender. The sauce should be reduced by cooking and served separately. Use a salad as garnish.

ROASTED CHICKEN

A regular chicken.—Salt.—Garlic.—Parsley.— Lemon.—White wine.—«Tocino».

Clean the chicken, remove the legs, neck and the gibblets and season it with salt, mashed garlic and parsley, a squirt of lemon and place it on an oven tray. Now add a good squirt of white wine, cover the chicken with thin slices of «tocino», place a few pieces of onion in the bottom of the tray and add a small amount of water to prevent it from burning. The chicken should be arranged in a similar way as the drawing.

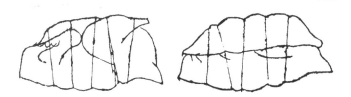

Put it in the oven, turning it only once in the middle of the roasting process and basting it with the sauce.

To serve the roasted chicken, it must be very hot and should be presented cut into serving pieces.

Remove the grease from the juice with a spoon, add a quarter of a cup of stock or water and bring it to boiling point, pass it through the sieve and pour part of this sauce over the pieces of chicken. The rest of the sauce must be served separately.

Garnish with hearts of lettuce, potatoes, etc.

ROASTED PHEASANT

The pheasant is cooked similar to the chicken and turkey.

Pheasant.—«Tocino».—Brandy.—Garlic.—Salt.

Clean the pheasant, season it with salt and mashed garlic and leave it for two days outside as in the case of the jacksnipes.

Tie the pheasant by the wings and legs as the chicken, sprinkle it with brandy, cover it with thin slices of «tocino» and put it in the oven adding a small amount of water to prevent it from burning and sticking to the tray.

When the pheasant is roasted, remove the slices of «tocino» and the string and serve in its own juice.

ROASTED TURKEY

The turkey is cooked as in the recipe for «Roasted chicken». It is served cut into pieces after removing as many bones as possible. Accompany with a lettuce salad.

ROE DEER

The roe deer is cooked similarly to kid or lamb.

STEWED PARTRIDGES

Partridges.—«Tocino» from ham.—Carrots.—A few leaves of different vegetables.—Garlic.—Parsley. Onion.—Laurel.—Salt.—Oil and butter.—Lemon.— Paprika.

Chop the «tocino», a small carrot per partridge, onion, a branch of parsley, one clove of garlic, a leaf of cabbage per partridge, etc. Place all this, seasoned with salt in a casserole and on top, put the partridges seasoned with salt and mashed garlic and parsley. Pour a good squirt of lemon and another one of oil on top of each partridge or smear them with butter. Add some stock or water to cook and sprinkle with paprika if desired. Cover the casserole tightly and place it to cook over strong fire.

To serve, the sauce must be passed through the sieve.

STEWED RABBIT

One rabbit cut into serving pieces.—One cup of olive oil.—Two carrots, sliced.—Six branches of parsley chopped finely.—Two cloves of mashed garlic.— One tbls. of flour.—Two cups of red wine.—One large onion, finely sliced.—Two leaves of laurel.— One tsp. of wild marjoram.—Salt and pepper to taste.

First brown the pieces of rabbit in olive oil. When the pieces are nicely browned add the onion, carrots, laurel, parsley, garlic, wild marjoram and season with salt and pepper. When all these ingredients look golden, add a tbls. of flour and let it brown a little as well. Add two cups of wine, let it boil for two minutes and allow everything to simmer with the pan covered, until the meat is tender.

STUFFED PIGEONS

They are cooked similar to «Stuffed chicken».

STUFFED TURKEY

This dish is prepared similar to the recipe for «Duck with asparagus» or the same as any other stuffed fowl. It is served cut into fine slices adorned with the stuffing. The sauce is served separately.

SURPRISE CHICKEN

One chicken.—Oil.—One regular carrot.—One regular onion.—Parsley.—Laurel.—Dry wine.—Spices if desired.—Mashed potatoes.—Grated cheese.

Clean the chicken and season it with salt, mashed garlic and parsley. Cut it into pieces and cook it with 2 tbls. of butter, a quarter of a cup of dry wine, one carrot, one onion, a few branches of parsley and a leaf of laurel.

When the pieces are cooked, place them in a mound and cover them with part of the mashed potatoes. The rest of the mashed potatoes are dyed very lightly with hard bolied egg yolks, tomato sauce, vegetable green, etc. and it is then used to adorn the dish.

Sprinkle with grated cheese and place it in the oven for a moment under strong heat. Serve the sauce separately.

TURKEY

The turkey with scaly and red legs is old, and the meat not as tender.

TURKEY STUFFED WITH TRUFFLES

This dish is prepared similar to «Hen stuffed with truffles». When it is cooked, you may pour over it a small amount of water in which you have previously dissolved some gelatin. Allow to dry and serve.

Canned goods
and cheeses

PRESERVED FRESH GRAPES

Tresh grapes may be preserved, first by choosing good clusters. These must be ri pe and should cleaned throughly removing anything that could harm or spoil the grapes.

Tie the clusters with strings and hang them separately and without touching the walls. You may also put them on a cloth instead of hanging them. Place them in a cool place protecting them against the sun. They can be preserved in this way for more than three months. The grapes take the form of raisins.

CANNED PIMIENTO

Choose the most healthy and ripest pimientos and clean them very well. Place them on a tray and insert them in the oven to roast, not too much, under strong heat. Remove them from the oven and peel them, discarding also the seeds.

Next, place them in clean jars covering them with oil and not shutting the jars until the oil has penetrated in all corners and the jars have been cooked in a double boiler at least for half an hour. Cover the containers immediately with paper dipped in alcohol and then with a second piece of paper so that it makes a perfect seal. The second piece of paper is tied around the mouth of the jar with a wet string.

If you are using bottles instead of jars, you must cut the pimientos in strips first, fill the bottle with oil, place the cork and cover it with wax so that the air does not penetrate through the pores.

Keep the jars or bottles in a cool place.

CANNED TOMATO

Choose ripe tomatoes but not soft ones. In a big casserole with boiling water, you add the tomatoes for a few minutes, then remove them from the boiling water and peel them placing them next in clean glass jars. Then pour salted boiling water into the jars making sure there are no air pockets and the tomatoes are covered. Cook them in a double boiler for two hours and close them firmly.

CHEESES

There are various classes of cheeses. The type and quality of the cheese depends on the class of milk from which it is made, the fermentation time, the environment, the temperature, etc.

The first thing that has to be done is to curd the milk. Each region makes its own class of cheese which vary according to the way they are dried, fermented, etc.

For example, to make the Galician cheese it is necessary to situate the cheese in a place where the temperature is 18 or 20° C or in the kitchen without excess heat.

First you filter the milk. It must be freshly milked, if not the milk must be warmed up a little. The milk is coagulated with curd which you can buy in a store along with instructions as to how it is applied and in what quantity. The curd is added to the milk and normally one tbls. is

142

added per quart. The milk is stirred well and then it is left to stand untouched until you can see that the milk is of solid consistancy by moving the pot gently. The milk should be curded in a porcelain container.

The excess liquid that has not settled (this is light green or yellowish in colour) is drained and the curded milk is placed in a cheese cloth and hung up to allow the liquid to drip from it. After a few hours it will be clear that it is well dried.

Fill the molds in which you intend to make the cheeses with the curded milk (these molds should be of a wicker type, that is with air holes to speed drying) and invert them frequently for two or three days. When the cheeses are well dried, qprinkle the surface and the sides with salt and leave them for another day, removed from their molds. The next day, turn them over and sprinkle the other surface with salt, letting them stand for another twenty-four hours. During this time, the cheeses should be placed on a wooden board.

The cheeses can now be left in a cool dry place.

FRUIT IN SYRUP

Prepare the fruit you are going to preserve, by washing it well, peeling it only if the skin is tough, cutting it through the center and removing the pits or the core, and removing any spots that there may be.

The containers in which you are going to cook the fruit should be of porcelain or stainless steel (copper and tin containers should not be used). The fruit is placed in the container with alternate layers of sugar. The first and last layer should be sugar. Let the fruit stand with the sugar from ten to twenty-four hours depending on the toughness of the fruit. After this time the fruit is cooked over high heat and it should be stirred continously to prevent it from sticking and so that all the impurities will be released and rise to the surface. The foam which forms should be skimmed off very thoroughly, because if anything is left in the fruit, it could cause fermentation and dis-troyit.

Cook the fruit until the liquid or juice that forms is thick like a syrup. If the syrup is too thick it will crystalize later on.

Allow the fruit to cool and pour it into the containers in which you intend to preserve it, which should be previously heated to prevent them from cracking. In each jar place a couple of tbls. of cognac. The fruit is left in the open jars for two or three days. After this time the jars are filled with syrup if they are not completely full and then closed tightly.

Proportions of sugar needed for various types of fruits cleaned and with pits or core removed.

For two pound of apricots	1 lb.	12 oz.	of sugar
»	»	»	» cherries	1 lb.	9 oz.	»	»
»	»	»	» plums	1 lb.	12 oz.	»	»
»	»	»	» strawberries	1 lb.	12 oz.	»	»
»	»	»	» gooseberries	1 lb.	12 oz.	»	»
»	»	»	» sour apples	2 lb.	3 oz.	»	»
»	»	»	» swett apples	1 lb.	12 oz.	»	»
»	»	»	» quinces	2 lb.	3 oz.	»	»
»	»	»	» oranges	2 lb.	3 oz.	»	»
»	»	»	» pears	1 lb.	9 oz.	»	»

PEACHES IN SYRUP

Cut peaches in half after they have been peeled and remove the pits. Place them in a jar and cover them with cold syrup. Close the jars tightly and boil them for 30 minutes. The water in which they are going to be boiled must be cold from the beginnig.

«PIMIENTOS MORRONES»

Four pounds of pimientos.—One quart of water.— Three and a half ounces of salt.—Oil.—Two jars of a little less than a quartsize.

Roast the pimientos to remove the skin and wash them in cold water. Cut the stalk off and remove the seeds.

Place them in the jars, boil the salt and water together for 5 minutes, then allow to cool and with that salted water cover the pimientos. Then add some oil to form a layer on top of about on fifth of an inch. Close tightly and keep in cool place.

STRAWBERRIES IN SYRUP

Clean and wash the strawberries, place them in a flask, pour some syrup up to the half way mark, close up tightly and boil the container for 10 minutes.

YOGURT

Buy in the store some «Yogurt ferment». It comes preparet in small jars and it is used to make yogurt (do not confuse this yogurt ferment with the curd used to coagulate the milk).

Boil the milk until it reduces its volume quite a bit to eliminate the water. Let it cool and when the milk is warm pour the yogurt ferment on top, stir gently and distribute this mixture into small containers. Allow to stand until everything is curded but not any longer.

Yogurt is one of the most nutritious foods. If you leave a small amount of yogurt to mix with milk and allow it to stand until the next day, you will always have yogurt.

Drinks

ALMOND REFRESHMENT

Mash the almonds, leave them in water for twenty-four hours, add the sugar you like and stir until it dissolves. Filter this and serve cold.

«CAP» OF FRUIT

Chop any kinds of fruit and mix them with lots of sugar. Add chopped ice, white wine, cider and a small amount of liquor (brandy, rum, etc.). To serve place a few pieces of fruit in each cup.

«HORCHATA» OF FRUIT

**One pound of chufas.—One quart of water.—Sugar.—
A pinch of cinnamon.—Half the rind of a lemon, grated.**

Clean the chufas from the earth they may contain and soak them in water for 10 hours. Mash the chufas three times mixing them with the water after each time, to make them release all the juice. Pass the mixture through the sieve once more and discard the residue. To the liquid add sugar, a pinch of cinnamon and the lemon rind.

LEMONADE

One half pound of lemons.—One third of a pound of sugar.—One quart of boiling water.

Cut the lemons into small pieces and mix them with the sugar in a container resistant to heat. Add a quart of boiling water, allow to boil momentarily and then to cool. Filter and serve.

«MACEDONIA» OR COCKTAIL OF FRUIT

Any kind of fruit may be used, peeled and cut into small pieces. Add a good amount of carbonic water and a little bit of liquor (brandy, anise, etc.). Next add good amount of sugar and let it stand until next day. Serve in cups.

«MAZAGRAN»

One glass of strong coffe.—A shot of brandy or rum.—A slice of lemon.—One half glass of sugar.—A piece of ice.

Mix everything, stir for five or more minutes, filter it and serve.

«PONCHE»

One half quart of milk.—A small cup of rum.—Two egg yolks.—Sugar.

Beat the egg yolks, sugar (the amount of sugar depends on the individual) and rum. Add the cold milk and mix thoroughly. You may add a little coffee if you like. Warm up to your particular taste.

REFRESHMENTS

The simplest ones are made with sugar or honey, water and juices of fruits. They may be accompanied with ice if desired. Serve them in cups or glasses with straws.

«SANGRIA»

A quart of white or red wine.—Three quarters of a quart of carbonic water.—Sugar.—Liquor.—Some fruit.

Mix the carbonic water and wine, then add the liquor (half a cup of brandy or any other liquor), and next the sugar you like. Stir well with some slices of orange and / or any other fruit you like.

STRAWBERRY REFRESHMENT

Mix strawberries and sugar in equal amounts, add a good amount of lemon juice and a pinch of clove. Boil until it thickens a lot, stirring continously. Filter it and keep it in a container. It should not be kept long. To use, mix it with water.

TOMATO, ORANGE OR LEMON REFRESHMENT

Put a tomato (without seeds), peeled orange or lemon in the blender. Add a small amount of water and sugar to taste.

WHIPPED MILK

One quart of milk.—Four egg whites.—Sugar.—Lemon.—Cinnamon.—Ice.

Boil the milk with a lemon rind. When the milk is cold, add the egg whites (which have been beaten until they stand in peaks) together with the necessary sugar to sweeten it. Mix very well and put it on ice to cool. Serve very cold sprinkled with cinnamon.

WINE REFRESHMENT

Mix the wine you like with some water, add a few slices of lemon, ice and sugar to taste.

Cakes and pastries

ALMOND CAKE

One cup of white almonds.—Two thirds of a cup of sugar (icing sugar to sprinkle on top of finished cake).—Three eggs,—Two tbls. of rum.—One half cup of flour.—A pinch of salt.

Preheat oven to 350° F. Beat the eggs and the sugar together until it forms a thick cream. The almonds should be ground until they have the consistency of powder or a fine paste and mix them with the flour and the salt. Add this mixture together with the eggs and the rum and blend it lightly.

The batter is then poured into the baking pan (8 in × 12 in.) which should be greased and sprinkled lightly with flour previously. The baking time is about twenty five minutes. To cool, turn the cake upside down on a cake rack or on a piece of wax paper sprinkled with icing sugar.

To adorn the cake, sprinkle it with icing sugar just before serving.

ALMOND CREAM

Three ounces of sugar.—Two egg yolks.—Five ounces of almonds.—A few drops of liquor if desired.

With three ounces of sugar and half this amount of water make a syrup. Let it cool and mix it with the mashed almonds and the beaten yolks. Next add the liquor if desired. Mix everything thoroughly until you get a fine cream.

ALMOND PASTE

Three and a half ounces of almonds.—Two eggs.— Two tbls. of butter. A small cup of flour.—Three and a half ounces of sugar.—Two tbls. of milk.—Lemon, cinnamon, vanilla, etc. essence if desired.

Mix the sugar with the melted butter and the two beaten eggs away from the fire. When this is well mixed, add the peeled mashed almonds and the milk. Next add the essence if desired and the flour. Mix everything well and now it is ready to use. You may use it as a filling for cakes, pastries, etc.

APPLE CAKE

Six tbls. of flour.—A tsp. of yeast.—Two eggs.
Six tbls. of flour.—A tsp. of baking powder.—Two eggs.

Peel five apples and cut them into pieces placing them to cook in a light syrup until they are half done. Reserve them for later use.

Melt the butter and add to it six or seven tbls. of sugar. When the sugar is melted, remove it from the fire and allow it to cool. Next add the beaten eggs mixing them well with the rest of the ingredients. Add the baking powder and flour stirring continuously until forming a fine and thick cream.

Caramel a mold and plce a layer of cream, another of cooked apples in syrup finishing with the rest of the cream.

Sprinkle with a good amount of sugar and place thin slices of raw apple on top, mounting one on top of the other starting from the center towards the outside. Sprinkle again with sugar and finally put it in the oven under medium heat.

«BAÑO DE CARAMELO»

Sugar.—Water.—Lemon.

Make a light syrup with the sugar and water. When you are removing it from the fire, add a few drops of lemon. Stir well. This syrup is used to adorn and brighten cakes, pastries, etc. This can be made in two different ways, by dipping the cake or pastry in the syrup or smearing the syrup on the cake with a brush.

«BAÑO DE CHOCOLATE»

Three ounces of chocolate.—Two tbls. of butter.— Sugar.—Water.—Flour.—One egg white.

Mix a tbls. of flour with about three ounces of water. Place on the fire and add the butter and chocolate (grated or in powder). Let it cook until the chocolate is melted and thick. If you do not like it so thick you may add some more water. Remove from fire, add an egg white (beaten until it stands in peaks) and since it hardens when cooling use it without letting it get cold. You may eliminate the egg white if you wish.

«BAÑO DE YEMA»

Syrup.—Egg yolks.

Make a syrup «a punto de hebra» (see recipe for syrup in this chapter). When it is done, remove it from the fire and when it sufficiently cooled add the egg yolks (one

152

yolk per every three ounces of syrup). Place it on the fire again until it gets the consistency you desire, stirring it continuously.

«BOCADO DE DAMA»

Six eggs.—One ounce and a half of water.—One half pound of flour.—One half gram of ammonium carbonate.—A tsp. of potato fecula or potato flour.

Beat the egg whites until they are fluffy and stand in peaks and then mix them with the beaten yolks. Nex add the rest of the ingredients and stir until you get an even and fine cream. Pour this cream in paper molds.

The molds should not be filled since the cream will rise in the oven. Place the molds in the oven under medium heat until the pastries are done.

BONBONS «AL KIRSCH»

Five «mantecadas» (recipe found in this chapter under «Mantecadas from Leon»).—Two egg whites.—Three ounces of grated chocolate and two ounces of powdered chocolate.—Three or four tbls. of icing sugar.—Two shots of Kirsh liquor.—Three and a half ounces of mashed almonds.

Crumble the «mantecadas» and mix them with the liquor, the almonds, the icing sugar, the powdered chocolate and with an egg white that has been previously beaten until it is fluffy and stands in peaks.

Form the bonbons in the shape you prefer and sprinkle them with the greated chocolate. Allow to stand for 10 hours. After this time place them in paper capsules.

«BORRACHINES»

One «bizcocho» (recipe to be founf in this chapter).—Syrup with sherry.

Cut a «bizcocho» into rectangular pieces. It should have been made quite thick. Make a syrup and add a squirt of sherry. Place the pieces of «bizcocho» upside down and cover them with the warm syrup. When this is done, turn them right side up and then they are ready to serve.

«BIZCOCHO»

Three eggs.—Three tbls. of flour.—Three tbls. of sugar.

If this recipe is to be used to make other pastries, you may increase it according to the amount you want to make.

Beat the egg whites until they stand in peaks. Beat the egg yolks separately and then mix the two together along with the sugar. The flour is added gradually so that the mixture will not fall. When everything is mixed thoroughly, it is poured into a mold of your preference previously greased. After the batter has been pured into the mold or molds allow it to rest for a few minutes before placing it in the oven. While baking the «bizcocho» should be covered with a piece of greased paper to prevent it from burning. The oven should be heated strongly, if not the flour will settle on the bottom and only the top will rise. The grased paper is a must, and should be replaced in this case by a fresh sheet when the other is burned.

When the «bizcocho» is done (it is tested by placing a toothpick or a knitting needle in the center and if it comes out clean the cake is done) remove it from the oven, allow to cool and remove it from the mold.

The molds should not be filled more than half as the «bizcocho» rises quite a bit.

BUTTER CREAM

To cream the butter knead it with your hands which should be moist or use a blending instrument. As you are kneading, add gradually sugar dissolved in hot water or syrup until it is of the consistency desired.

This cream is used to adorn cakes, pastries, etc.

«BIZCOCHO DE SOLETILLA»

Five eggs.—Three and a half ounces of sugar.— Three and a half ounces of flour.—Icing sugar.— Orange or lemon concentrate.

Beat the egg whites until they stand in peaks. Beat the egg yolks separately with the sugar and a few drops of lemon or orange concentrate, until it forms a fine even cream. Add the beaten egg whites and the flour carefully. Place tablespoonfuls of the batter on a cookie sheet in an oblong shape. The dough should be well spaced as it rises a lot.

Let the cookie sheet stand for 10 minutes before placing it in the oven and then bake them. The «bizcochos» should be watched carefully as they bake very quickly.

«BIZCOCHO» OR BISCUITS «EMBORRACHADOS»

Make a syrup with three parts of water and one of sugar. Cook this stirring continuously for ten minutes and after pour the syrup over «bizcocho» or other biscuits before the syrup has a chance to cool.

A squirt of liqour may be added to the syrup to give it more flavour. The «bizcocho» may be parted when serving by cutting it with a hot knife, to prevent it from crumbling.

«BIZCOCHO» WITH MERINGUE

One half pound of «bizcochos».—Light syrup.— Liquor or sherry.—Three beaten egg whites.—Sugar.— Lemon.

155

The «bizcochos» (previously baked) are placed on a cookie sheet in parallel lines and covered with the hot syrup. To the beaten egg whites, add sugar and lemon to your taste. Cover the «bizcochos» with this egg mixture.

They may be sprinkled with cinnamon. Place them in the oven until the meringue in golden and then remove them allowing them to cool.

Serve them cold. They may be served with custard.

«CANUTILLOS»

With the «hojaldre» paste (recipe given in this chapter) form hollow tubes by rolling the dough around a cilyndrical mold. Place them in the oven.

When baked and cooled these «canutillos» may be filled with the cream of your preference.

CARAMEL

One half pound of sugar.—Four ounces of water.— One tsp. of glucose.—Essence and colorants if desired.

Disolve the sugar and glucose in water and make a syrup «a punto de bola» or «a punto de caramelo» (see recipe for syrup). Then add the essence and colorant, stir it and pour the syrup on a greased tray. Before it gets hard cut the caramels with a mold or with a greased knife.

Another variation is to add grated chocolate to the mixture when you are making the syrup.

To make chocolate cream caramels, cook iqual amounts of sugar, butter, grated chocolate and honey. When the mixture has the consistency desired, pour it on a tray, cut the caramels and when they are cold dry them with a cloth before wrapping them with paper.

CHOCOLATE BONBONS

Three ounces of first class chocolate.—Two tbls. of roasted almonds or hazelnuts.—Three tbls, of powdered sugar.—One egg white.—Chocolate to dip them in.

Mash the hazelnuts and chocolate until it has the consistance of a powder. Mix with a beaten egg white. Then mold the bonbons as you like.

Dip them in thick chocolate and allow them to dry in a cool place for 12 or 14 hours.

CHOCOLATE CREAM

Six ounces of water.—Six ounces of chocolate or six tbls. if it is powdered.—A tsp. of flour.—Three tbls. of butter.—Two or more tbls. of sugar.

Mix the water and flour and then add the chocolate, butter and sugar. Allow it to cook briefly stirring continously until you get a thick cream.

It is used mainly to cover «Gypsy's arm» (see recipe in this same chapter).

CHOCOLATE «DE MERIENDA»

One half pound of sugar.—Three and a half ounces of cacao.—One tbls. of glucose.—Two tbls. of butter.— One ounce and a half of milk.—Three and a half ounces of hazelnuts or almonds.

Mix everything except the almonds and cook until it thickens and acquires the desired consistency. Then add the cracked almonds. Pour the mixture on a cold surface previously greased with oil from sweet almonds and let it cool for a few minutes. Before it cools completely cut it in squares or rectangles.

«CHURROS»

One cup of flour.—One cup of water.—A squirt of lemon.—One tbls. of oil.—One half tsp. of salt.— Sugar for sprinkling.—Abundant oil to fry them in.

First the water, a squirt of lemon, salt and a tbls. of flour should be brought to a boil. The flour is all added at once and the ingredients are stirred until the dough is smooth and thick. Let the dough cool and then put it in a «churrera», which is a type of squirt gun where the dough is pressed through. You can use a cake decorator with a hole about one half inch wide. The dough is dropped into abundant hot oil, each «churro» being about four inches long.

Test the oil first, because if the oil is not hot enough, the «churros» will separate and if it is too hot they will burn. They are golden brown when done. Allow the oil to drain well from them, sprinkle them with sugar, and serve them hot.

«Churros» are used to dip in hot chocolate or coffee.

COCONUT EGG YOLKS

Grated coconut.—Syrup «de hebra fuerte» (see recipe for syrup in this chapter).

Make a syrup «de hebra fuerte». Remove it from the fire and add enough coconut to thicken it and be able to make balls with the mixture.

If the mixture does not blend well, it is because the syrup was not prepared properly or because too much coconut was added. If this is the case, add and egg white without beating it and mix it slowly until everything blends.

Place the paste in small paper capsules.

COCONUT «FLAN»

A cup of milk or water.—A cup of sugar.—Five ounces of grated coconut.—Five eggs.

With the water and sugar make a syrup and allow to cook until the volume is reduced to half. Then mix the coconut with it.

Beat the eggs and mix them with the syrup and coconut.

Caramel a mold and allow it to cool. Pour the mixture in it and place it in a double boiler until it sets completely (about two hours). If you insert the mold in a pressure cooker, the time will be reduced to a quarter of an hour. Allow it to cool and invert the mold on a plate, tray, etc.

COFFEE CREAM

Three tbls. of flour.—Half a quart of milk.—One tbls. of butter.—Coffee.—Sugar.

In a small pot, brown lightly two tbls. of sugar. Then add the milk and three tbls. of ground coffee. When the sugar has dissolved and boiled, filter the liquid through a fine and wet cloth.

To this coffee with milk, add now three tbls. of flour and the butter. Place on the fire and stir continously. When the cream is cooked (To test it, take a small amount and put it on a wet plate. It should come off easily when cold) add the sugar to your taste. Now it is ready to use.

CREAM FOR TARTS «NATI»

Six ounces of sugar.—Three and a half ounces of raw almonds.—Three or four egg yolks.—Two or three «bizcochos», crumbled.—Rum or cognac.

Make a syrup «a punto de perla» (see recipe in this chapter) with six ounces of sugar, one and a half of water and the mashed almonds. Allow to cool a little and then add the yolks stirring contin ously. When everything is homogeneous, remove it from fire and add the «bizcochos» and a squirt of rum or brandy. Mix thoroughly and then it is ready to use.

«CUCURUCHOS DE HOJALDRE»

«Hojaldre».—Cream.—Molds with a cone shape.

The «hojaldre» pate is rolled and cut into fine strips. These are rolled around the mold and placed on a greased oven tray. Insert them in the oven under strong heat. When they are brown, remove the molds carefully and fill the «cucuruchos» with cream or marmelade.

EGG YOLK CANDY

Syrup «a punto de hebra» (see recipe in this chapter).— Egg yolks.

Mix three egg yolks per every six ounces of cold syrup. When they are well blended, put the mixture on the fire until it thickens considerably.

Let it cool and make balls which are dipped in icing sugar. Place them in paper capsules.

FIRST CLASS «MAGDALENAS»

Three eggs.—Three tbls. of flour.—Five tbls. of sugar.—Two tbls. of butter.

Beat the egg whites until they stand in peaks, then mix them with the beaten egg yolks, sugar and very slowly with the butter and flour. Knead it well until everything is well blended and uniform. The dough is like a thick cream. Place the dough into special paper molds and insert them into the oven under light or medium heat.

«FLAN»

Per every egg use: Three ounces of milk.—One or two tbls. of sugar.—A pinch of cinnamon if desired.

Caramel a mold (this is done by melting sugar in a mold, spreading it evenly on the sides so that it forms a caramel shell inside).

Beat the eggs adding the sugar, milk, and the cinnamon if desired. Mix it thoroughly and pour it in the mold. Place the mold in a double boiler until the «flan» sets and then in the oven without removing it from the water, until it gets solid. Allow to cool and place the «flan» on a plate by inverting the mold.

«FLAN DE SUIZOS»

Two eggs.—Three «suizo» buns (see recipe in this chapter).—Sugar.—Milk.—Cinnamon.

Beat the eggs. Mash the buns in a cup with a little milk. Add the sugar you like to the eggs and mix them with the buns and milk. This mixture is poured in a mold prepared as in the former recipe. Place the mold in a double boiler until the eggs set. Allow it to cool and then empty the mold by turning it upside down.

«FLORONES Y FRISUELOS»

One egg.—One cup of milk.—Flour.—Salt.—Sugar.—Oil.

Beat the egg, add the milk, a pinch of salt and then the necessary flour to form a thick cream. Put a small amount of this cream in hot oil. If the cream divides itself in pieces, add more flour to it until it does not break when put in hot oil.

To make «frisuelos», fry in hot oil (not too hot to prevent the «frisuelos» from burning) the batter shaped as a spiral. This can be done by using a tablespoon full with the batter and letting it fall into the oil. When the «frisue-los» are brown, place them on a tray and sprinkle them with sugar. To make «florones», the dough must be a little thicker and you also need a special mold. (This mold is a small cup shaped in various forms with a long handle so that you will not get burned when using it). Heat the mold by placing it in the hot oil, then take some of the dough with the mold but without filling it up. Next place the mold with the dough in hot oil and in a few seconds the dough will release itself from the mold. You need a little bit of practice with the mold. If it is too hot, the dough will not stick to it and if it is cold, the dough will not release itself when frying.

Fry them, drain the oil from them and place them on a tray sprinkling them with sugar.

FRIED MILK

Half a quart of milk.—Four or five tbls. of **flour.**—One or two tbls. of butter.—Lemon **rind.**—Cinnamon.—One or two eggs.—Sugar.—Oil.

Dissolve the flour in cold milk and to this add some lemon rind and a pinch of cinnamon. Cook this with the butter stirring it continously. Let it cook for at least fifteen minutes and when it is almost finished, add the amount of sugar you wish.

Once it is cooked, pour it on a damp tray to cool and at this time remove the lemon rind. When it is cool, cut it into serving squares which are dipped in flour, egg and then fried in oil. Drain the oil from the squares or rectangles and sprinkle them with sugar before serving.

GYPSY'S ARM

A «bizcocho», long and not too thick.—Chocolate cream.—«Pastry cream».

To make the «bizcocho» (see recipe in this chapter). The recipes for «Pastry cream» and «Chocolate cream» can be found in this chapter also.

When the thin «bizcocho» is still warm, spread it with «pastry cream» and roll it immediately before it gets cold since then it would break. Wrap the «bizcocho» in white paper and allow it to cool. When it is cold, remove the paper, place the «bizcocho» on a tray and pour on top of it some «Chocolate cream».

Decorate the «Gypsy's arm» with a cream made with butter and sugar pressed through a cake decorator.

162

HALF MOONS

Cut wide strips of «hojaldre» paste. (Recipe found in this chapter). The paste should be about a quart of an inch thick. Fold the strips in an angle or trim them in the shape of half moons. Coat them with egg white (beaten) and place them briefly in the oven.

«HOJALDRE»

One half pound of flour.—One half pound of butter.—A pinch of salt.—A small cup of water (the amount of water can not be determined exactly since it depends on the kind of flour being used).—Flour to sprinkle the dough.

The «hojaldre» is one of the pastes more difficult to make. Follow strictly all the advices since the smallest detail will prevent the paste from turning out flaky.

Sprinkle flour on a cool flat surface, and then make a pile of flour with a hole in the center. Dissolve the salt in the water and pour it in the flour slowly with your left hand and at the same time mix this with your right hand using only the fingers. Do it as fast as you can using only the indispensable water. When this is done, take pieces of the dough and press them with the palm of your hand in a circular motion (avoid kneading) until the dough has formed a ball of a soft consistency. Make a few slits in the ball with a knife, sprinkle it with flour, cover it with a wet cloth and allow to stand for 15 or 20 minutes.

The butter must be kept in a cold place. Wrap it in a ser-

viette sprinkled with flour and knead it briefly to make it softer so that it will mix with the dough without warming it up.

Take the ball of dough after it has been standing for 15 minutes and place it on a flat surface previously sprinkled with flour. Press the ball with the palm of your hand until you have formed a square (see drawing)

Spread the center section of the dough evenly with butter and fold the corners of the dough to the center like an envelope (see drawing).

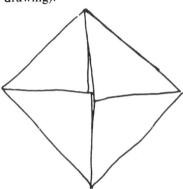

With a rolling pin, this folded dough is rolled out in all directions keeping its square shape until it is as large as it was before it was folded. In doing this be careful that the butter does not escape as this will ruin the «hojaldre».

Again sprinkle the table and the dough with flour. Fold the left and right edges of the dough over each other so that you have a rectangle with three layers (see drawing).

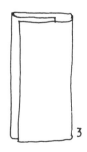

This rectangle is then rolled out into a square again using the rolling pin. The table, rolling pin and dough should be sprinkled with flour when it is necessary to prevent the dough from sticking. Turn the square upside down on the table and then fold the four corners to the center as described previously, and once again roll this out in all directions keeping its square shape until it is as large as it was before it was folded.

Allow the dough to rest for 15 minutes.

Repeat this process two more times allowing the dough to rest between them for 15 minutes.

When all this has been done, the «hojaldre» may be cut into the sizes and shapes necessary for the particular use.

«Hojaldre» needs a short baking time in the oven as it burns easily.

«HUEVOS MOLES»

Six egg yolks.—Ten tbls. of sugar.—Four tbls. of water.

The yolks should be very clean without membranes or egg white. Mix all the ingredients together. Put it in the fire stirring contin ously and removing it from the fire occasionally until it gets like a thick cream.

Prepare as many little molds as egg yolks and caramel them. (To do this, see recipe for «Flan» in this chapter.) Pour the thick cream in the molds and when it is cold, empty the molds on a glass plate.

«MANTECADAS» FROM LEON

Two eggs.—Three ounces of refined oil.—Five tbls. of sugar.—Four tbls. of flour.—One halft tsp. of baking powder.

Beat the egg whites until they stand in peaks and then mix them with the beaten egg yolks, sugar, oil, flour and baking powder. Mix thoroughly and place a big tablespoon-

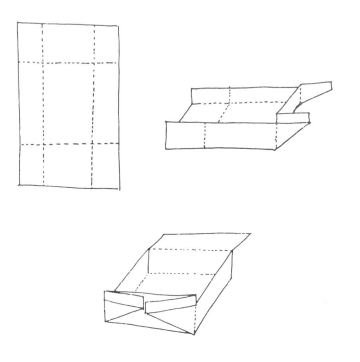

ful of the thick cream in each paper capsule. To make the capsules proceed as ilustrated in the drawing:

When this is done, place them in the oven under medium heat. This recipe makes about two dozen.

MARZIPAN «AMPARO»

> **One half pound of lightly toasted almonds, powdered.—
> One pound of first class potatoes.—One pound of
> sugar.—Five egg whites beaten until they stand in
> peaks.**

Wash the potatoes and cook them with their skin in boiling water. When they are cooked, peel them before they cool and mash them well. The mashed potatoes are mixed with the rest of the ingredients except the egg whites. Reserve a small part of the egg whites to paint the marzipan.

When this is done, mix the rest of the egg whites with the previous mixture, until everything is well blended. When the paste is homogeneous make a marzipan, that is to say, like a big round «bizcocho». Paint it with the egg white you reserved and place it in the oven on a greased paper.

Before molding the paste, you may stuff it with canned fruit in their syrup.

«MEDIAS NOCHES»

«Medias noches» are small buns made with the same paste as the one used for making «Suizos» (see recipe in this chapter). The «medias noches» are sliced in two and filled with cheese, butter, ham, etc.

«MERENGUES»

One half pound of sugar.—Four egg whites.—One half glass of cold water.—Two tbls. of icing sugar.

Make a syrup «a punto de bola» (see recipe in this chapter) with the half pound of sugar and the water.

Beat the egg whites until they stand in peaks and add the icing sugar to it. Next mix the egg whites with the warm syrup and allow to stand for 10 minutes. Put this mixture in a cake decorator with an opening at least one inch wide. Squeeze the «merengues» through the cake decorator on to a cookie sheet previously covered with a piece of wet paper. Place the cookie sheet with the «merengues» into the oven under low heat. Before the «merengues» get brown, remove them from the paper and place two and two together by the flat surface. Serve them cold on a glass plate.

«MILHOJAS»

In order to make a «milhojas» it is necessary to make previously a «hojaldre» (see recipe in this chapter) cut in rectangles about three inches long and one and a half wide and not too thin. Place them in the oven and after you remove them, join two or three by putting some «pastry cream», «merengue», etc. in between.

«NATA MONTADA»

«Nata montada» is a well beaten cream from the milk to which you may add some sugar, or egg whites. This is similar to whipped cream.

«NATILLAS»

Per every egg yolk, use: three ounces of milk, a tbls. of sugar. You may also add a pinch of cinnamon if you like.

Mix the yolks with the milk, sugar and a pinch of cinnamon if desired. Put it over low heat stirring continously until it thickens. It must not boil. The «natillas» are served a little bit cold. They may also be poured on biscuits, «bizcochos», etc.

NEGRO HEADS

«Rice with milk al caramelo» (see recipe in this chapter).—«Baño de chocolate» (see recipe in this chapter).—«Merengue» (see recipe in this chapter).

The rice with milk should be thick and cold. Mold it as a ball and place it on a glass plate. Pour the «baño de chocolate» on top and adorn the dish with «merengue». You may put two almonds as eyes and cherries as the mouth.

PASTRY CREAM

Three tbls. of sugar.—Two tbls. of flour.—One or two beaten eggs (better without the egg whites).— Lemon rind.—Boiling milk.—Cinnamon.

Mix everything and allow to cook for ten minutes stirring continously under low heat. Then pour the cream on a tray, sprinkle with cinnamon and place it in the oven to keep it warm while you prepare the cake, pastries, etc. on which you are going to use the cream.

«PETIT CHOUX»

A cup of flour.—A cup of water or milk.—Three eggs.—Salt.—Lemon.—Oil.—Syrup.—Any cream you like.

Boil the water or milk with a bit of salt and a piece of lemon rind. When it starts to boil, add the flour, stir for a few moments and remove it from the fire. Keep stirring it, add the eggs one by one without beating them, mixing them well with the dough. Do not add the next egg until the former is well blended with the dough. You may add a pinch of yeast. Allow to rest briefly. The same as with the «Wind puffs» (see recipe in this chapter) make small balls with two teaspoons and fry them in abundant hot oil without browning them too much.

Prepare a cream you like, «pastry cream», yolk cream, etc. and stuff the «petit choux» with it. To do this it is necessary to empty carefuly the raw cream that did not fry in the interior of the balls and replace it by the cream.

The upper parts of the «petit choux» are painted with a thick syrup.

«PICATOSTES O TORRIJAS»

Slices of day old bread.—Milk.—Sugar.—Egg.—Oil.

Cut slices of bread, dip them in sugar water, then in beaten egg and fry them in abundant hot oil. Drain them well and sprinkle them with sugar.

PLUM CAKE

Three eggs.—One tbls. of butter.—One half tsp. of baking powder.—Six tbls. of flour.—Raisins.—Canned fruit in their syrup.—Sugar.

Beat the egg whites until they stand in peaks and mix them with the beaten egg yolks, baking powder, a handful of raisins, flour and a squirt of liquor. Blend everything thoroughly and then put it in a greased mold. Insert it in the oven until baked.

RICE WITH MILK «AL CARAMELO»

A cup of rice.—Three ounces of water.—Two cups of milk.—Three tbls. of butter.—Sugar.—Stick of cinnamon.—Lemon.—Salt.

Clean and wash the rice and add it to the boiling water for a couple of minutes. Add the butter, cinnamon to taste, a slice of lemon and milk, allowing it to continue cooking over low heat. The milk should be added gradually as the amount required depends on the kind of rice being used. Add salt to taste. When the rice is almost cooked, add sugar to sweeten it to your taste remembering that the dessert surface will be convered with sugar later on. Complete cooking the rice.

When the rice is tender, pour it on a tray and let it cool a little. When the surface begins to feel solid, sprinkle it well with sugar. With a bar of red hot iron burn the sugar in whatever patern you desire. Serve it warm.

«ROSCÓN DE REYES»

Dough similar to that of «Suizos» or «Hojaldre».— Canned strips of pumpkin in their syrup or canned cherries and oranges.

Make a ring shape with the dough and insert a prize wrapped in greased paper inside of the dough. Paint the upper surface of the ring with beaten egg and adorn it with strips of pumpkin, cherries or oranges. Place it in the oven until it is done.

Serve it on a paper doily.

170

«SACHEPOS»

Seven egg yolks.—Three egg whites.—Two tbls. of sugar.—Three tbls. of flour.—Syrup.—Cinnamon.

Beat the egg whites and the egg yolks separately, then mix them and beat them again. Next add two tbls. of sugar and three tbls. of flour blending it very well without beating it. Prepare paper cones with a greased paper and place them in a mold as ilustrated:

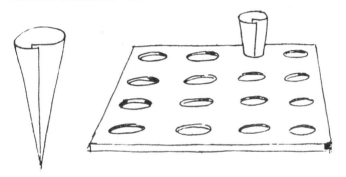

Place a paper cone half filled with cream in each hole of the mold. Place them in the oven. When they are done, take them out of the oven and remove the paper cones. The «sachepos» are dipped in a light syrup and placed in paper capsules as illustrated:

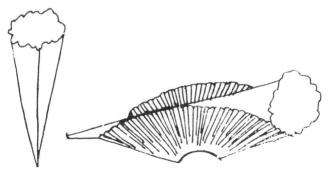

SAINT BONES

Marzipan paste.—Marmalade for filling.

Roll the marzipan paste around sticks (make sure these sticks do not affect the flavour of the marzipan) and place them in the oven to dry and harden. Take them out of the oven and remove the sticks. Fill these cylinders with marmalade or with any other cream you like.

Almond paste may also be used instead of marzipan paste.

SELECTED «TORRIJAS»

Slices of molded bread (better if it is one or two days old).—Butter.—Marmalade.—Egg whites beaten with sugar and grated lemon rinds until they stand in peaks.

Smear butter on the slices of bread. On top of the butter, spread marmalade and finish with a layer of the egg white mixture. Place them in the oven until the egg whites are lightly browned.

SOUFFLÉ IN BRANDY

Egg whites.—Egg yolks.—Icing sugar.

Beat the yolks adding sugar to your taste. Beat the egg whites and mix them with the yolks. You may also add a pinch of vanilla or cinnamon. This is the souffle.

Place some «bizcochos» on several earthenware plates. Top the «bizcochos» with souffle and then insert them in the oven for a few minutes. Remove them from the oven and pour some hot brandy on top of each one setting the brandy on fire. Serve immediately.

SPUN EGG

Syrup.—Egg yolks.

Make a syrup «a punto de hebra fina». (See recipe in this chapter.) Spread a layer of this syrup on to an earthenware tray and place it over the heat. The very cleaned egg yolks are pressed through a sieve (very fine) over the syrup so that it comes out in threads. (This operation should be done as fast as possible.)

With a skimmer or fork, very quickly remove the egg yolk threads and pass them under cold water before placing them on a plate. The spun egg is frecuently used in making pastries, cakes, tarts, etc.

SUGAR «GLASS»

Sugar.—Rice flour.

Grind regular sugar into a fine powder on a flat surface. To be more economical two parts of sugar and one part of flour may be used. This is similar to the bought icing sugar.

«SUIZOS»

One egg.—Three ounces of refined oil.—A big cup of milk.—Flour.—Six or seven tbls. of sugar.—Less than half a tsp. of salt.—One tbls. of baking powder.

Mix the milk, baking powder, sugar, egg and oil all together and blend it well. After it has stood for a while, add the necessary flour to make a batter which will not stick to your fingers but will still be fine and soft and allow it to stand wrapped in a cloth after you have sprinkled it with flour. The dough should rest in a warm place until it is double in size.

The dough is then formed into small buns (they will rise a lot) and slit in the center. The buns are painted with egg or egg white. You may sprinkle them with sugar. Place the buns in a hot oven until done.

This recipe makes 20.

SYRUP

Syrup is a mixture of a large amount of sugar and a small amount of water. The thicker you want the syrup the longer you have to cook it.

173

The syrup of course gets thicker when it cools and you can test it removing a small amount, letting it cool and testing it between your fingers.

The success of the syrup is influenced a lot by the care taken in skimming. The syrup should be skimmed continously so that it will be completely transparent and without bubbles and crystals.

The syrups will be numbered according to their thickness. The thinnest syrup will be number one.

1. «Light syrup». This syrup will cover the holes of a skimmer when it is dipped in the syrup.

2. Syrup «de hebra fina». Wet your fingers with cold water, take a sample of the syrup between two fingers and for the syrup to be of the right consistency threads should form between your fingers when they are separated.

3. Syrup «de hebra fuerte o gruesa». The test is equal to that in number two except that for this one, the threads of syrup will be much thicker and stronger.

4. Syrup «punto de perla». You will notice the pearls forming as the syrup is boiling. When testing with your fingers, the resistance will be stronger than before.

5. Syrup «punto de goma o de bola». When a sample is taken between your fingers it should form a ball. Also if a skimmer is dipped into the syrup and you blow through the holes, long white bubbles will form.

6. Syrup «punto de lámina». This syrup is ready when a small ball made with the syrup, will be crisp and crack when bitten.

7. Syrup «punto de caramelo». This is the thickest syrup. After this point the sugar will burn.

To make the syrup trasparent, add an egg white (without beaten it) while the syrup is boiling. Stir it and you will notice that the egg white will set and turn black from the dirt of the sugar. The egg white is removed by sieving the syrup and it will then be clear.

«TARTALETAS»

«Hojaldre».—«Almond paste» (the recipes for these two dishes can be found in this chapter).

174

Prepare small molds to make the «tartaletas» and cover the inner walls of them with the «hojaldre» paste. Then fill the mold with rice or beans to prevent the dough from rising. Place them in the oven. When they are done, take them out of the oven and remove the rice or beans. Fill the molds now with «almond paste», place them again in the oven under high heat and remove them when they are slightly brown.

The «tartaletas» may also be filled with marmalade, fruit in syrup, etc.

«TOCINO DE CIELO»

Two and one half cups of sugar.—Lemon rind (one quarter of a lemon).—Three quarters of a cup of water.—Sixteen egg yolks.—One whole egg.— One half cup of sugar.

Caramel a ring mold (done by heating sugar until it is light brown and lining the mold with it). The two and a half cups of sugar, water and lemon rind are simmered in a saucepan for half an hour. The syrup should be tested often to see if it is ready and this is done by dipping a spoon in it and holding it vertically over the pan. If the last drop forms a thin thread, remove it from the fire and let it cool to normal room temperature. The egg yolks and the whole egg should be blended (but not beaten) and as you continue to stir them, gradually add the cold syrup and sieve the mixture. Put the caramelized mold on top of a plate in a pan of water which is hot but not boiling, to prevent it from burning the bottom. Next add water to one third the height of the mold and pour in the custard.

Remove any foam that is present, cover it as tightly as possible and simmer it for an hour approximately. The foam that forms in cooking should be skimmed off occasionally. The «tocino de cielo» should be served removed from the mold and slightly chilled.

175

WALNUT BREAD

**One egg.—One half pound of sugar.—Flour.—Milk.—
Three and a half ounces of raisins.—One half pound
of walnuts.—A small tbls. of yeast.—Salt.**

Beat the egg, add half tsp. of salt and the sugar beating
it well. Next, add the milk (one half quarter in which you
have dissolved the yeast). Finally add the raisins without
seeds, the chopped or mashed walnuts and flour to form
a paste not too thick. Blend it well, spread it with the pin
roll, take the ends and fold them towards the center, spread
the dough again and repeat the process several times. Allow
the dough to stand in a warm place for at least half an hour
wrapped in a cloth sprinkled with flour. Make a few slits
in the dough and place it in the oven covering it with a
greased paper to prevent the dough from burning. The oven
must be very hot. Remove the bread from the oven when
done and allow it to cool wrapped in cloths for several
hours.

WIND PUFFS

**A cup of flour.—A cup of water.—A pinch of salt.—
Two eggs.—Cinnamon.—Icing sugar.—Oil.**

Boil the water, when it starts to boil add a pinch of salt
and the flour stirring continously near the fire until you
obtain a uniform paste. You must work a lot with the batter
but do not add more water. When the dough is uniform,
remove it from the fire and add the eggs one by one. When
one egg is perfectly blended, add the next, mix everything
thoroughly and allow it to rest for a few minutes.

In a frying pan with abundant hot oil, fry small portions
of the dough taken by using two teaspoons. Move the
frying pan continuously but do not touch the «wind puffs»
as they will turn by themselves when one side is browned.
You must have a cover or lid for protection since as the
dough fries, it starts to expand until it bursts. The oil
should be hot but not in excess. Drain the oil from the
puffs and sprinkle them with icing sugar and cinnamon
previously mixed together.

176

Pastes and biscuits

«ALMENDRADOS»

One cup of toasted almonds.—Two thirds of a cup of sugar.—Three egg whites, four if the eggs are small.—One dozen almonds for decoration.

The oven should be preheated to 350° F. Grind the almonds to a fine paste. The almond paste is then mixed with the sugar and the egg whites beaten just enough to blend. This mixture should be of a consistancy thick enough that when it is dropped from a spoon, it will hold the shape of a cookie.

Heaping tablespoonfuls of the batter are then dropped onto a cookie sheet and each cookie decorated with half an almond. The cookies are baked until they are browned, which takes from 12 to 15 minutes. The cookies will get crips as they cool.

This recipe makes approximately two dozen cookies.

CAT TONGUES

One egg.—Two and a half tbls. of sugar.—Two tbls. of butter.—Three tbls. of flour.—Grated lemon rind, vanilla essence, cinnamon, etc.

Beat the sugar and butter and then add the beaten egg and a little bit of the grated lemon, vanilla essence, etc. Mix thoroughly and add the flour (the amount of flour may change according to the quality of itself). The resulting batter must be like a thick cream. With a spoon, place small portions of the cream in a long shape on a cookie sheet. These portions must be well spaced since they widen a lot.

Place them in the oven and remove them as soon as the edges brown. To detach the tongues from the cookie sheet you may use a knife with a rounded tip. The tongues are delicious but very fragile.

CHRISTMAS FIGURES

The Christmas figures are made with a «marzipan paste». (The recipe may be found in the former chapter under «Marzipan Amparo»). Make the figures you like with the paste and place them in the oven for a few minutes. The figures are served on wafers varnished with egg white.

«COQUITOS»

Two eggs.—Seven tbls. of sugar.—Ten ounces of grated coconut.

Beat the eggs, add the sugar, mix it well and then add the coconut blending all together. Place small mounds of the mixture on a greased paper and insert them in the oven for a few minutes under medium heat until they are lightly browned.

CREAM BISCUITS

A cup of flour.—Two tbls. of butter.—One tbls. of pork lard.—Ten ounces of sugar.—A tsp. of baking powder.—One egg.—Two ounces of almonds.

Mix the flour, baking powder and salt with your fingers. The pork lard and the butter are beaten well with the sugar until they form a cream. Then add the beaten egg, a tbls. of water and mix everything thoroughly. When the mixture is uniform add the flour. The resulting batter should be thin but not in excess. If the batter is too thin you may add more flour. Roll the paste out and cut circles of it with a glass. Paint them with beaten egg and place a raw almond in the center of the circle sticking it with a little bit of honey. Place them in the oven. They should be removed as soon as they start to get lightly browned.

DOUGHNUTS FROM REINOSA

One half pound of flour.   One half pound of butter.— A shot of anise.—Salt.—One egg yolk.

Half of the total amount of flour is mixed with the butter and kneaded well. Wrap it in cloth and put it in a cold place for half an hour.

The rest of the flour is mixed with the anise, a pinch of salt and a small amount of warm water. Add more flour if necessary so that the batter does not stick to your fingers. Roll the batter out in a square shape. On top, roll the other batter you made in the beginning in a smaller square shape.

Fold the edges towards the center and roll them out. Repeat this operation several times (the procedure is similar to the one used with «hojaldre»). Roll the dough out finally and cut thick strips. With these strips make the doughnuts and place them in the oven. When they have been removed and cooled, they are painted with syrup and sprinkled with icing sugar.

DOUGHNUTS OF SAN ISIDRO

One half pound of flour.—Five tbls. of sugar.—One tsp. of baking powder.—Two eggs.—Two tbls. of brandy.—Three tbls. of refined oil.—Two or three anise seeds.

Beat the eggs well and mix them with the sugar, baking powder, the cold oil and two or three anise seeds, roasted and mashed. Blend all the ingredients thoroughly and then add the flour to form a soft dough.

Roll the dough out and cut circles with a glass. With your wet finger make a hole in the center to give them the shape of doughnuts. Allow them to rest in a warm place for an hour. After this time, paint them with egg or egg white and place them in the oven under strong heat but being careful they do not burn.

This recipe makes about 15 doughnuts.

«EMPIÑONADOS»

«Marzipan paste» (the recipe may be found in the former chapter under «Marzipan Amparo»).—Piñons. One egg white.

Blend the marzipan paste with the piñons. With this paste make small portions shaped as half a moon. Paint them with beaten egg white and insert them in the oven for a moment.

«HOJUELAS»

One egg.—One tbls. of oil.—Flour.—Salt.—Syrup or honey.

Beat the egg white and the yolk separately and then mix them together, adding a pinch of salt and the necessary flour to form a soft batter that does not stick to your fingers. Roll it out so that it is thin and cut it into irregular triangles. Fry them in oil.

When they have been fried, paint them or dip them in a thick syrup or in honey mixed with a little bit of water.

ORANGE PASTES

One half pound of flour.—Four ounces of sugar.— Four ounces of butter.—Two ounces of preserved orange.—One egg white.

Beat the butter and then mix it with the egg white previously beaten until it stands in peaks. Next, add the orange well chopped, stir it and finally add the flour. Knead all the ingredients well and form pastes with a tongue shape. Place them in the oven.

Remove them from the oven when they are done and before they cool, dip them in a mixture made with an egg yolk and three tbls. of water. Allow them to dry before serving.

«PALMERAS»

«Hojaldre».—Syrup.

Cut the «hojaldre» paste into strips. Fold both ends towards the center and place them in the oven. When they are done, remove them from the oven and dip them in syrup «a punto de perla» (see recipe in the former chapter). Allow them to dry.

«PALOS DE BARCELONA»

Two eggs.—Five tbls. of sugar.—Lemon or lemon concentrate.—Three tbls. of refined oil.—One half tsp. of baking powder.—Flour.—Icing sugar.—Oil.

Beat the two eggs and mix them with the oil, sugar baking powder and a good squirt of lemon juice. Blend every thing until the sugar dissolves. Next, add the flour to form a soft paste that does not stick to your fingers. Take small portions of the dough and roll them between the palms of your hands so that the ends are pointed and thin and the center thick.

Fry them in abundant hot oil (not too hot). Remove the pan occasionally from the fire so that the oil does not get too hot while frying, the pieces of dough will expand and a few slits or cracks will appear in the center. Drain the oil well, allow them to cool a little and sprinkle them with icing sugar.

«POLVORONES»

Two cups of flour.—One cup of sugar.—One cup of melted pork lard.—Icing sugar.

Knead all the ingredients except the icing sugar make small portions with the batter in the shape of circles (these should be quite thick.). Place them briefly in the oven under low or medium heat. Dip them or cover them with icing sugar. Wrap them in a thin paper (tissue or onionskin) with the edges cut as illustrated:

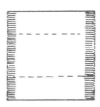 

«POLVORONES» OF HAZELNUT

The same recipe as above with less sugar a handful of mashed hazelnuts. Place them in the oven very briefly as they harden very fast.

«ROSCAS LEONESAS DE TRANCALAPUERTA»

Six eggs.—Three ounces of refined oil.—Three tbls. of strong brandy, rum, etc.—Flour.—Vinegar.—Sugar.—Salt.

Beat the six egg yolks and mix them with an egg white previously beaten. Add the oil slowly and then the brandy. Next the sugar a pinch of salt and mix everything well. Then add the necessary flour to make a thick paste but not a batter. Put tablespoonfuls of the paste on a white paper (they must be apart because they rise quite a bit). With your wet finger make a hole in the center of the paste to shape it as a doughnut. Place them in the oven to bake and remove them as soon as they start to get lightly brown.

Beat the egg whites, add sugar to taste and a tbls. of lemon juice. With this mixture paint the «roscas» on one side and insert them in the oven to dry under very low heat. When they are dry, remove them from the oven, paint the other side and repeat the operation.

SIGHS

Eight tbls. of flour.—Five tbls. of butter.—Four tbls. of sugar.

Mix the butter with the sugar and then add the flour. Mold the paste with your hands in the shape of biscuits. Place them in the oven and remove them when they start to get lightly brown. They break easily. Sprinkle them with icing sugar.

TEA PASTES

One pound of flour.—A quarter of a pound of butter.— One egg yolk.—Two ounces of milk.—Lemon, vanilla, or any other essence.—A pinch of salt.

Mix all the ingredients and knead well. Roll out the dough and cut it into the shape you desire and then bake them in the oven after you have painted them with egg white, egg or water.

YOLK DOUGHNUTS

Six egg yolks.—Six tbls. of sugar.—Two tbls. of butter.—Two tbls. of brandy, rum, etc.—Flour.

First beat the egg yolks and then add them to all the other ingredients except the flour which is added gradually until you have made a soft and tender dough. Form the dough into the shape of doughnuts and bake them in the oven. When they are done, coat them with a syrup «a punto de caramelo» (see recipe in the former chapter) to frost them.

Cakes, icecreams and «turrones»

ALMOND CHEESE

One half pound of raw, peeled, and perfectly mashed almonds.—Eight fine «bizcochos».—Nine egg yolks.— Three egg whites.—One pound of sugar.—A shot of brandy.—Cinnamon or vanilla.

Beat the egg whites until they stand in peaks. The egg yolks are beaten separately and then the yolks and the beaten egg whites are mixed with the brandy, sugar, cinnamon or vanilla, mashed almonds and the «bizcochos» which should be well crumbled. Place this mixture over low heat, stirring it and let it cook a little. When you can see the bottom of the pan by stirring the cheese, pour the mixture in a mold greased with butter. Allow it to cool for twenty four hours. To remove the «almond cheese» from the mold, place the mold in hot water and the cheese will then slip out easily.

ALMOND «TURRÓN»

One half pound of sugar cubes.—One half pound of honey, the whitest honey possible.—Five egg whites.—Ten ounces of almonds, lightly toasted and parted.

The honey and the sugar are mixed over the heat. When you see that the sugar starts to melt add the egg whites previously beaten until they stand in peaks. Stir continuously so that it does not get brown. At the same time remove the pot from the fire. It should turn out as white as possible. Next add the almonds and continue stirring. Place the pot over high heat for a moment. When the mixture is going to acquire the consistency of «punto de caramelo» (see recipe for Syrup under Cakes and Pastries) remove it from the fire and pour it in molds previously lined with white paper first and wafers on top.

BISCUIT CAKE

Round or square biscuits depending on how you like the cake.—Syrup.—Creams.—«Merengue».

Prepare the cream of your preference (pastry cream, marmalade, etc.). Place a layer of biscuits on a round tray which have been previously dipped in hot syrup. Place a tbls. of the cream you prepared on top of each biscuit. Cover the cream with another layer of syrup coated biscuits and place a tbls. of a different cream on top of each biscuit. Finally place a layer of syrup coated biscuits.

Cover everything with «merengue» and adorn it with almonds, chocolate, etc.

CHOCOLATE ICECREAM

One half pound of chocolate.—A quart of milk.— Six egg yolks.—Sugar.—Cinnamon.

Mix the milk with the grated chocolate and place it to cook. Beat the egg yolks, add the sugar you like to them and pour this mixture onto the milk and chocolate, stirring continuously until the chocolate is completely molten. Remove the pot from the fire a little to prevent the mixture from burning. When all the ingredients are well blended, allow

186

it to cool stirring it without stopping. Place it in the freezer.
You may add more milk if you desire.

«HOJALDRE» CAKE

To make this dish you need two pieces of the «hojaldre» paste (see recipe for «Hojaldre» in the chapter of Cakes and Pastries). Place them in the oven separately after you have rolled out the dough in the shape you prefer. Make a «pastry cream» or any other you like and cover one of the «hojaldres» with it putting the other one on top. You may also cover this one with cream if you like. Adorn this dish like any other cake.

If you do not put any cream on top of the second «hojaldre», you must paint it with syrup or sprinkle it with icing sugar.

ICECREAM «DE NATA»

Cream from milk.—Sugar.—Fruit juice, chocolate, coffee, etc.

Whip the cream, add sugar to your taste and the fruit juice, chocolate or coffee. All the ingredients must be sweetened with sugar. Blend well and place the mixture in the freezer.

LEMON ICECREAM

A quart of water.—Juice from two large lemons.— Six egg whites, beaten until they stand in peaks.— The rind of a lemon, grated.—Sugar.

Boil the water for ten minutes with the lemon and the sugar you like. Allow it to cool and then add the egg whites. Place the mixture in the freezer.

MILK ICECREAM

Milk.—Cinnamon or vanilla.—Sugar.

Cook the milk with some cinnamon or vanilla and the sugar you like to sweeten it. Boil for five minutes and allow to cool. Then place it in the freezer or between ice.

«MOKA» CAKE

A round «bizcocho».—«Coffee cream» (see recipe under Cakes and Pastries).—Syrup.

Make a round «bizcocho» of the thickness you prefer. Cut it in disks if it is very thick or only in two if it is regular. Fill it with the «coffee cream» and also cover the sides with it. Adorn with crushed almonds, cream, etc.

ROYAL CAKE

Nine egg yolks.—Three egg whites.—Three tbls. of butter.—Three tbls. of flour.—Grated lemon.—Eleven ounces of ground raw almonds.

Beat the egg whites until they stand in peaks. Beat also the egg yolks separately. Grind the almonds with the sugar, mix all the ingredients, place them in a greased mold covered with another greased paper and insert it in the oven under medium heat. Adorn it as you prefer.

STRAWBERRY CAKE

One pound of strawberries.—One pound of sugar.— «Bizcochos de soletilla» (see recipe under Cakes and Pastries).—Icing sugar.

Wash and clean the strawberries, then mash them with the sugar. In a carameled mold (see recipe for «Flan» under

Cakes and Pastries) put a layer of strawberry cream and another of «bizcochos de soletilla» alternating until the mold is filled. Allow it to stand for more than an hour and then remove it from the mold. Sprinkle it with icing sugar when serving.

STRAWBERRY ICECREAM

One pound of strawberries.—An orange.—Six ounces of sugar.—Half a quart of water.—One half glass of cream from the milk.—Icing sugar.

Reserve the best strawberries (one third) for later use. The rest is washed and cleaned, then mashed with the sugar and the orange juice and it is allowed to rest for more than an hour.

After this time, add the water stirring it to dissolve the sugar. You may add more water if you think it is necessary. Place it in the freezer. Beat the cream from the nilk or use whipped cream instead.

To serve, place the icecream in cups or on plates, cover it with whipped cream and top it with the strawberries you reserved. These strawberries must be dipped in a hot and thick syrup for a good while, then allow them to cool before they are ready to serve.

«TURRÓN DE GUIRLACHE»

Sugar.—Toasted and parted almonds.—Lemon.

With sugar and water make a syrup «a punto casi de caramelo» (see recipe for «Syrup» under Cakes and Pastries) and when it is lightly brown, add a few drops of lemon and the almonds. Put it immediately on a greased cold surface. Before it cools completely cut it into bars of four inches by one.

«TURRÓN» FROM ALICANTE

Two pounds of honey.—One pound and one third of sugar.—Four egg whites.—Four pounds of almonds, lightly browned.—A few drops of anise.

Make a syrup «a punto de caramelo» (see recipe for «Syrup» under Cakes and Pastries) with the sugar and three ounces of water. Heat the honey on the fire and when it is liquid mix it with the syrup blending it well. Place the mixture on the fire until it gets the consistancy of caramel.

At this moment, add the almonds (parted), a few drops of anise and the beaten egg whites. Mix all the ingredients thoroughly and pour the mixture in molds previously covered with wafers and white paper.

«TURRÓN» FROM JIJONA

One pound of honey.—Three and a half ounces of sugar.—One half pound of almonds.—One third of a pound of hazelnuts.—One third of a pound of piñons.— Three egg whites, beaten until they stand in peaks.

Place the almonds and piñons in boiling water and remove the skin from them. You may toast them lightly if you want. Grind them as fine as possible, mixed with the sugar.

Melt the honey on the fire and mix it with the sugar, almonds, piñons and egg whites. Blend everything thoroughly and pour it into molds lined with white paper and wafers on top. Place some weight on top and leave it, the longer the better.

«TUTTI-FRUTTI» ICECREAM

It is prepared similarly to «vanilla icecream». When you are going to freeze it, add natural or canned fruits finely chopped.

VANILLA ICECREAM

A quart of milk.—Ten egg yolks.—Sugar.—Cinnamon, vanilla or lemon.—One tbls. of butter.

Boil the milk for ten minutes with the butter, cinnamon, vanilla or lemon and the sugar you like. Allow it to cool and then add the beaten egg yolks very slowly. Put this mixture in a double boiler and when it is about to boil, remove it from the boiler. Put it through the sieve and allow it to cool, stirring it one in a while with a wooden spoon. Place it in the freezer.

Fruits

«ALMENDRAS GARAPIÑADAS»

One pound of almonds.—One pound of sugar.—One tbls. of water.

Make a syrup by melting the sugar and the water together. When this is done, add the almonds and stir them continously until they are coated with the sugar and light brown in colour. To cool place them spread out on a sheet of paper on your kitchen counter. You should separate each almond before they cool.

ALMONDS

Almonds are very nutritious. They are used very frequently to make cakes, pastries, etc. To remove the skin from them, place them in boiling water for two or three minutes, then remove them from the water and they will peel easily. In the oven they toast quickly. To grind them it is necessary to add something to them (sugar, a little bit of water, etc.) since if not, they transform into oil.

ANGEL'S HAIR

Pumpkin.—Sugar.

Cut the pumpkin into two pieces and clean it by removing hard hilums and seeds. Place it in a casserole, cover it with water and boil it for about half an hour. Allow it to cool in the same water but before it cools completely peel it, and take the pumpkin hilums or threads and place them in cold water. Leave them in the water until next day. Then drain them and dry them and place them to cook with the same amount of sugar and half that amount of water, stirring it for about fifteen minutes. Allow it to cool. Next day place them to boil again adding more water and sugar if necessary for another fifteen minutes. Allow it to cool and repeat the operation the next day, always cooking it in the same casserole. When the pumpkin starts to get brown then it is ready to remove from the fire. Allow it to stand for several days in a cool place.

APPLE CAKE

Three and a half ounces of butter.—Three and a half ounces of sugar.—Half a tsp. of yeast.—Three and a half ounces of flour.—Two eggs.—One pound of good soft apples.—Icing sugar.

Mix the butter, sugar, flour, two eggs and the yeast dissolved in a tbls. of milk. Blend this mixture until you get a fine and even batter. Take a flat and round mold and line it with half of the batter after the mold has been greased.

Peel the apples, cut them in thin slices (descarding the core) and place them in the center of the mold. Cover them with sugar and then with the other half of the batter. Place the mold in the oven under strong heat and allow it to cook.

To see if the cake is ready, stick a knitting needle in it and if the needle comes out clean the cake is ready. It is convenient to cover the cake with a greased paper to prevent it from burning.

When the cake is cold you may sprinkle it with icing sugar.

APRICOTS IN SYRUP

Two pounds of healthy and ripe apricots.—Two pounds of sugar.—One half quart of water.

Wash and clean well the apricots. Place them in a casserole with water. When the water starts to boil remove them from the boilding water and place them in fresh water for about three hours. After this time, place them in the casserole where they are going to be cooked with the water and sugar. (Amounts of these two ingredients are given in the first paragraph of the recipe). Cook until you see that the apricots are tender and soaked with the syrup.

Remove them from the fire and allow them to cool.

BANANAS

Bananas do not have to be kept in refrigerators as the green bananas keep very well wrapped in paper and placed in a dark place.

CHERRIES IN SYRUP

Two pounds of sugar.—Two pounds of cherries.

Wash the cherries well and remove their stems. The pits can be removed with a special instrument for removing the pits or with a hair pin. Place the hair pin through the hole where the stem was, twist it and the pit will come out easily. Cleaned and with the pits removed, they sould be left in water for a few hours. Place the cherries in a casserole containing enough water to cover them and cook them for five minutes. Remove the cherries and place them quickly in fresh water for another two hours.

In a separate casserole make a syrup with the sugar and a cup of water, let the syrup cool a little and then add the cherries to it, well drained, allowing them to cook without breaking themselves. Once the cherries are cooked, remove them from the fire and place them in a fresh place to cool.

CHESTNUTS

Cook the peeled chestnuts for ten minutes in a pressure cooker with a small amount of water seasoned with salt. When they have been cooked, cool them quickly.

If the chestnuts are not peeled previously they will take quite a bit longer to cook.

CHESTNUT CAKE

Two pounds of chestnuts.—One tbls. of butter.—A small amount of sugar.—Four egg yolks.—Three quarters of a cup of milk.—Anise.—Salt.—Corn starch.

First wash the chestnuts and place them in boiling water without peeling them and with a small amount of salt. When the chestnuts are tender, peel them and mash them. Boil the milk and while it is still hot add the sugar and butter and let it cook for a few minutes. When this is done, mix it with the chestnuts, a few anisee, the egg yolks and a tbls. of corn starch. Let this mixture cook for two minutes, stirring it and then pour it into a mold previously greased and even better sprinkled with bread crumbs as well. Bake it in the oven for a few minutes so that it will set completely. Remove it from its mold and serve it.

CHESTNUTS IN SYRUP

Chestnuts.—Syrup.—Salt.

Peel the chestnuts by first soaking them in warm water for a few hours and then removing their skin. Cook the peeled chestnuts in boiling water containing a small amount of salt. When they are cooked, cook them again for another 10 minutes in a light syrup so that the chestnuts may absorb it. Once they are well soaked in the syrup, let them cool and serve them.

CHESTNUT SOUFFLÉ

One and a half dozen chestnuts.—One half dozen egg whites.—Two cups of milk.—One quarter of a tsp. of salt.—Two tbls. of butter.—Four tbls. of sugar.—One tsp. of vanilla.—Four egg yolks.

To remove the skins from the chestnuts, slit them half way around with a knife and place them in a hot until they open. They are then easily peeled. These chestnuts are now simmered until they are tender, in one tbls. of sugar, vanilla and milk. When this is done, mash them or put them through a blender until they are in a cream form. Add the butter, egg yolks and remaining sugar, mixing well. Heat this slowly for a couple of minutes so that the flavor may be absorbed throughout. Remove from the heat and when it has cooled completely add the beaten egg whites. Next it is poured into a buttered soufflé dish and baked for twenty minutes at 425°F. Serve immediately

«DULCE DE HIGOS»

Two pounds of figs.—Two pounds of sugar.—Lemo rind.

Choose ripe figs, pinch them in several places and place them in fresh water for two days changing the wate once in a while. The container with the figs must be covere with a clean cloth.

After this time, place the figs in fresh water with th lemon rind and cook them for ten minutes. Remove ther to another container with fresh water and leave ther until next day. Then drain them and dry them with a clotl With the sugar and half a quart of water make a syrup, coo the figs in it until they get transparent, allow them to coc and then they are ready to be preserved.

«DULCE DE MELÓN»

One melon.—Sugar.

Peel the melon by removing a thick rind and leaving only the ripest meat. Remove the seeds and hilums that may be present. Cut it into pieces. Add now half of its weight of sugar and let it stand for three hours. After this time, place it on the fire to form a syrup. When the syrup starts to get a golden tone in colour, remove the pot form the fire. Allow it to cool and it is then ready to be preserved.

«DULCE DE MEMBRILLO»

Use equal amounts of quinces and sugar.

First the quinces are peeled and boiled in cold water for half an hour. Remove the core, mash it and then weigh it. Now add and equal amount of sugar and place the mixture in a heavy pot. Cook this over moderate heat until it separates from the bottom and sides of the pot, which takes from 15 to 30 minutes and then pour it into a loaf mold to set. When it is solid, remove it from the mold and store it in waxed or foil paper. It will keep for months and may be served with cheese as a dessert or with toasts for breakfast.

FIGS, PEARS, GRAPES, CHERRIES IN SYRUP

Cook the fruit in syrup for three or four minutes. If you are preparing grapes, remove them with a skimmer, allow them to cool a little, peel them, and with a hair pin remove the seeds.

Pears should be peeled before cooking. Cherries are also removed from the syrup similarly to the grapes and their pits removed. When this is done, place them again in the syrup and continue cooking them until they are tender.

When the fruit has cooled, you may serve them or preserve them as you wish.

197

FRIED BANANAS

Bananas.—Butter.—Icing sugar.

The bananas are cut into slices or lengthwise and then fried in butter. Drain the butter well and sprinkle them with liquor or sherry and then with icing sugar. Serve them with biscuits or a yellow sponge cake.

FRUIT JUICE

Wash the fruit well and mash it after you have removed any impurity or imperfection. Place the mashed fruit in a cheese cloth and squeeze it to allow the juice to come out. You may add some sugar or lemon juice if desired.

GRAPES DESSERT

«Bizcochos» (see recipe in former chapters).—One pound of grapes.—Four eggs.—Sugar.—Milk.— Butter.—Grated chocolate.

Place a layer of «bizcochos» on an earthenware tray and then the grapes on top (you may place them whole or cut in half to remove the seeds). Beat the egg whites and yolks separately and then mix them together, add sugar to your own taste and half a quart of cold milk. Pour this mixture over the grapes and «bizcochos», place on top a few small pieces of butter and sprinkle everything with grated chocolate. Place it in the oven momentarily.
Serve it warm or cold.

«MACEDONIA» OF FRUIT

Any fruit you like.—Sugar.—Lemon.—Whipped cream.

Clean the fruit and cut it into small pieces. Cover them with orange juice and a small amount of lemon juice.

Add sugar to taste. They are served in cups covered with whipped cream with a cherry in the center.

PEACHES IN SYRUP

Peaches.—Raspberries.—Ground almonds.—Sugar.— Icecream.

The peeled peaches are cooked as the «Apricots in syrup» (see recipe in this chapter) until they are tender. Place a layer of icecream on a tray. Place the cold peaches on top and cover them with a think layer of raspberries. Sprinkle with the ground almonds.

PEARS IN SYRUP

Peel them and cook them in syrup for ten minutes. Place them in jars, cover them with a light syrup and close the jars tightly. Place them for twenty minutes in a double boiler.

PLUM MARMALADE

Two pounds of plums.—Four ounces of water.—Two pounds of sugar.

Clean the plums, cut them in half and remove the pits. Place them in water and cook them until they are tender, then add the sugar and cook for ten minutes stirring continously. Allow it to cool and then preserve it.

PLUMS IN SYRUP

Plums.—Sugar (the same weight as plums).

Wash the plums and prick them with a needle. Place them to cook in boiling water until they rise to the surface.

As they come up to the surface, remove them from the boiling water and place them in fresh water leaving them for one day. After this time place them on a cloth to dry.

With the sugar and half that amount of water, make a syrup and then add the plums. Put them on the fire. When the syrup starts to boil, remove the pot from the fire and allow it to stand until the next day. Repeat this operation for three or four days until the plums are cooked. To preserve them, they must be cold.

STRAWBERRIES

Strawberries should not be washed or cleaned until they are going to be used. They are washed in cold water to remove the dirt. To remove the stem, hold it as close to the base as possible, twist it two or three times and then pull.

STRAWBERRIES WITH CREAM

One pound of strawberries.—One half pound of «Bizcochos de soletilla» (see recipe in former chapters).—Sugar.—One half pound of cream.

Wash the strawberries well and cut them into slices. Place alternate layers of «bizcocho» and strawberries, starting and finishing with a layer of «bizcocho». Sprinkle sugar between the layers. Keep it cold and before serving adorn it with cream and a few strawberries.

STRAWBERRIES WITH MILK

Wash the strawberries and cut them in half. Place them in a deep tray and cover them with milk and sugar. Leave them in this mixture for two or three hours before serving stirring it occasionally so that the sugar will dissolve.

STRAWBERRIES WITH ORANGE

They are made exactly as «Strawberries with milk» but putting orange juice instead of milk.

Glossary of spanish words

Aceite.—Oil, most of the time Olive oil.
Aceitunas.—Olives. There are several kinds.
Ajo.—Garlic.
A la Americana.—American style.
A la Bilbaína.—Bilbao style. City of the northern coast of Spain.
A la cazuela.—A casserole dish; type of stew
A la crema.—With cream.
A la Flamenca.—Flamenco style.
A la gabardina.—Covered with batter.
A la Griega.—Greek style.
A la importancia.—No special meaning. It could be translated by «importance style».
A la Italiana.—Italian style.
A la jardinera.—Gardener style.
Al ajillo.—Prepared with garlic sauce.
Al ajo arriero.—A muledriver. Prepared with garlic.
A la marinera.—Sailor style. Prepared like fishermen do.
A la molinera.—Miller's wife style.
A la montañesa.—Mountain style.
A la plancha.—Broiled, grilled.
A la Vitoria.—Vitoria style. City of Spain.
Al batín.—Covered with batter.
Albóndiga.—A meat ball.

Albondigón.—A meat loaf.

Alcachofa.—Artichoke.

Al caramelo.—With caramel.

Al horno.—Baked.

Aliñar.—To season.

Ali-oli.—Sauce made with garlic and olive oil.

Al Jerez.—In sherry.

Al kirsch.—A liquor.

Almendra.—Almond.

Almendrados.—With almond.

Almendras garrapiñadas.—Sugar-coated almonds.

Almíbar.—Syrup.

Al nido.—In nests.

Al plato.—Plate. Prepared in a plate.

Amparo.—Name of a woman.

Anca.—Haunch.

Anchoas.—Anchovies.

Angula.—Grig.

Arroz.—Rice.

Asado.—Roasted.

Atún.—Tunafish.

Au gratin.—Toasted gilded.

Ave fría.—Lapwing.

Avellana.—Hazelnut.

B

Bacalao.—Codfish.

Baño a la yema.—Syrup with yolk.

Baño de caramelo.—Syrup with lemon.

Baño de chocolate.—Molten chocolate.

Baño María.—Bath of boiling water. Double boiler.

Becada.—Jacksnipe.

Bechamel o besamel.—White sauce made with milk, flour and butter.

Berenjena.—Eggplant.

Besugo.—Sea bream. Any blue fish can be used in recipes calling for this fish.

Biftec.—Steak.

Bizcocho.—Yellow sponge cake.

Bocadillo.—A sandwich.
Bocado de dama.—Type of pastry.
Bola.—A ball.
Bollo.—Cake.
Bonito.—Tunafish.
Boquerones.—Fresh anchovies. Any small fish can be used as a substitute.
Borrachines.—Type of pastry with some spirits added.
Brazo.—Arm. Anything shaped like an arm, i.e. a cylindrical cake.
Buding.—Pudding. A casserole dish.
Buñuelo.—A puff, or fritters.

C

Cacerola.—Casserole. Dish prepared in a casserole.
Café.—Coffee.
Calabacín.—Zucchini squash.
Calabaza.—Pumpkin.
Calamar.—Squid.
Caldereta.—Fish stew.
Caldo.—Bouillon.
Callos a la Madrileña.—Tripe, Madrid style.
Campesino.—Country style.
Campero.—Country style.
Canela.—Cinnamon.
Canelones.—Sheet of white paste.
Canutillos.—Cylindric molds. Anything shaped like a cylinder.
Canutos.—Another way to call the cylindric shaped pastries.
Cap.—Cup.
Cardo.—Thistle.
Carne en fiambre.—Meat to eat cold.
Carne picada.—Ground beef.
Casero.—Homemade.
Castaña.—Chestnut.
Cazuela.—Casserole. Type of stew.
Cebolla.—Onion.
Cerdo.—Pork.
Champaña.—Champagne.

Champiñones.—Mushrooms.
Chanfaina.—Dish prepared with lights.
Chartreuse.—Type of liquor.
Chilindrón.—Dishes prepared with ham, tomatoes and pimientos.
Chipirones.—Squids.
Chocha.—Woodcock.
Chorizo.—Ground seasoned meats (pork), shaped like sausages are very popular in Spain.
Chufa.—A nut-like root used to make horchata.
Chuleta.—Chop.
Churros.—A fried doughnut very typical in Spain.
Clara de huevo.—An egg white.
Cochinillo.—A suckling pig.
Cocido.—Boiled. Also national dish of Spain made of leguminous vegetables.
Cocina.—Kitchen.
Col de Bruselas.—Brussel sprout.
Coliflor.—Cauliflower.
Compota.—Stewed fruit.
Conejo.—Rabbit.
Copa.—Wine glass. A cup.
Cordero.—Lamb.
Cordero lechal.—Milk fed lamb.
Cordero pascual.—Spring lamb.
Conservas.—Preserves or canned goods.
Consomé.—Consommé.
Coquitos.—Coconut pastes.
Corzo.—Roe deer.
Crema.—Cream.
Crema pastelera.—Cream filling for pastry.
Croquetas.—Croquettes.
Cucuruchos de hojaldre.—Puff paste cone shaped.
Cuello.—Neck.

D

Delicias.—Delights. Something tasty and delicious.
De merienda.—For lunch. Merienda is one of the Spanish meals around 6 p.m.

De nata.—Of skim.
De soletilla.—No special meaning. Type of sponge cake.
De vigilia.—Of vigil, hence without meat.
Dulce.—Sweet.
Duquesa.—Duchess.
Duro.—Hard.

E

Emborrachados.—Made with liquors.
Empanada.—A type of meat turn over.
Empanadilla.—A type of pie.
Empanados.—Breaded.
Emparedados.—Sandwich.
Empiñonados.—With pine cone seeds.
En adobo.—Tanned.
Encapotados.—Overcast. Type of hard boild egg dish.
Encebollados.—With onion.
En fiambre.—To be eaten cold.
En pepitoria.—Special way to prepare a chicken dish.
En rollo.—Rolled.
Ensaimada.—Type of bun.
Ensalada.—Salad.
Ensaladilla.—Potato salad.
Entremeses.—Hors d'oeuvres. Cold buffet.
Escalfado.—Poached.
Escalope.—First class fillet.
Escudella.—Typical Catalonian dish.
Espagueti.—Spaghetti.
Espárragos.—Asparagus.
Espinacas.—Spinach.
Estofado.—Type of stew.

F

Fabada.—Dish from Asturias.
Faisán.—Pheasant.
Filete.—Fillet.
Flan.—Custard.

Flan de suizos.—Special kind of custard.
Flores.—Flowers.
Florones.—Pastries with flower shape.
Foie-gras.—Goose liver.
Fresas.—Strawberries.
Fresones.—Large strawberries.
Frío.—Cold.
Frisuelos.—A type of pastry.
Frito.—Fried.
Fritura.—A fried dish.

G

Galleta.—Biscuit.
Gamba.—Shrimp.
Garrapiñado.—Covered with a hard coat of sugar.
Gazpacho.—A cold soup typical of the south of Spain.
Gelatina.—Gelatin.
Glas.—Ground sugar.
Glaseadas.—With ground sugar.
Granizado.—Made with shaved ice.
Gratinado.—Toasted. Made with grated cheese.
Grosella.—Gooseberry.
Guarnición.—Garnish.
Guindilla.—Chili pepper or Guinea pepper.
Guirlache.—Brittle almond.
Guisantes.—Peas.
Guisado.—A stew.

H

Haba.—Broad bean.
Harina.—Flour.
Hígado.—Liver.
Higo.—Fig.
Hojaldre.—Puff paste.
Hojuela.—Paste with the shape of a leaf.
Horchata.—Refreshing drink made from «chufas».
Horno.—An oven.

Huevos.—Eggs.
Huevos moles.—A kind of pastry made with molds.

Jamón.—Ham.
Jerez.—Sherry.
Jijona.—From Jijona. City of Spain.
Judías.—Beans.
Judías verdes.—String beans.

Lacón con grelos.—Typical dish from Galicia.
Langosta.—Lobster.
Langostinos.—Prawns.
Leche.—Milk.
Lechuga.—Lettuce.
Lenguado.—Sole or flounder.
Liebre.—Hare.
Limón.—Lemon.
Limón verde.—Lime.
Lomo.—Loin.

Macarrones.—Macaroni.
Macedonia.—Fruit cocktail.
Magdalenas.—Type of buns.
Mantecada.—A kind of pastry made with butter.
Manzana.—Apple.
Marina.—Name of a woman.
Marisco.—Seafood.
Marrón glacés.—Dessert made with chestnuts.
Mayonesa o mahonesa.—Mayonnaise.
Mazagrán.—Special drink made with coffee and liquor.
Mazapán.—Marzipan.
Mechar.—To lard.

Medias noches.—Types of buns.
Mejillones.—Mussels.
Melocotón.—Peach.
Membrillo.—Quince.
Menestra.—Vegetable dish.
Menudillos.—Giblets.
Merengada.—Whipped.
Merengue.—Meringue.
Merluza.—Hake. Any other big white fish can be used in recipes calling for this fish.
Meuniere.—Special dish of flounder.
Miel.—Honey.
Milhojas.—Pastry made with puff paste.
Moka.—A tipe of coffee cake.
Mollejas.—Sweetbreads.
Morcillo.—Type of meat.

N

Nabo.—Turnip.
Naranja.—Orange.
Nata.—Cream, skim.
Nata montada.—Well beaten cream.
Natillas.—Type of custard.
Nido.—Nest.
Nueces.—Walnuts.

O

Olla.—A pot.
Ostra.—Oyster.

P

Paella.—Rice dish typical from Valencia.
Paellera.—Shallow pan for cooking paella.
Palmeras.—A type of paste.
Palos de Barcelona.—A type of paste from Barcelona.

Parrilla.—A grill.
Pasta.—Paste.
Pastel.—Pie.
Pastel de carne o pescado.—Pâté.
Patata.—Potato.
Pato.—Duck.
Pavo.—Turkey.
Pechuga.—The breast of a fowl.
Pepino.—Cucumber.
Pepitoria.—Dishes prepared with egg yolks and almond.
Pera.—Pear.
Perdices.—Partridges.
Pescado.—Fish.
Picatostes.—Bread soaked in milk and fried.
Pierna.—Leg.
Pichones.—Pigeons.
Pimienta.—Black pepper.
Pimiento morrón.—A type of pimiento.
Piña.—Pineapple.
Pisto.—A vegetable casserole.
Plátano.—Banana.
Plato.—Plate. Dish.
Pollo.—Chicken.
Polvorones.—A type of paste.
Ponche.—Punch.
Postre.—Dessert.
Potaje.—A vegetable dish.

Q

Queso.—Cheese.

R

Rabioles.—Ravioli.
Rebozada.—Covered with batter.
Relleno.—Stuffed.
Repollo.—Cabbage.
Riñones.—Kidneys.

Rollo.—A roll. Something with cylindrical shape.
Ron.—Rum.
Rosbif.—Roast beef.
Roscas Leonesas de Trancalapuerta.—A type of doughnut from Leon.
Roscón de Reyes.—A type of pastry for Christmas.
Rosquilla.—Doughnut.

S

Sachepos.—A type of pastry, cone shaped.
Sal.—Salt.
Salchicha.—Sausage.
Salsa.—Sauce.
Salsa picante.—Highly seasoned sauce.
Salteado.—Sauteed or sauté.
Sandía.—Watermelon.
Sangría.—A typical refreshing drink made with wine and fruits.
Sesos.—Brains.
Sesos huecos.—Soft brains.
Sidra.—Hard cider.
Solomillo.—Sirloin.
Sopa.—Soup.
Sopa Juliana.—Herb soup.
Suizos.—A type of bun.

T

Tallarín.—Noodle.
Tapas.—Spanish appetizers.
Tarta.—Cake.
Tártara.—Tartar.
Tartas Nati.—A type of cake.
Ternera.—Veal.
Tocino.—The white fatty part of pork that is found directly under the skin.
Tocino de cielo.—A special kind of pastry.
Tomate.—Tomato.

Torrijas.—Bread soaked in milk and fried.
Tortilla.—An omelet.
Tostado.—Toasted.
Trucha.—Trout.
Trufa.—Truffle.
Trufado.—Stuffed with truffles.
Turnedo.—Steak made from the beef fillet.
Turrón.—Typical Spanish candy during Christmas, made
with almonds and nuts.
Tutti-frutti.—Ice cream with chopped fruit in it.

U

Uva.—Grape.

V

Variados.—Assorted.
Verde.—Green.
Vieiras o conchas de peregrino.—A type o seafood.
Vinagre.—Vinegar.
Vinagreta.—Vinegar sauce.
Vino.—Wine.
Vino blanco.—White wine.
Vino tinto.—Red wine.
Vol-au-vent o pastel de hojaldre.—A type of pastry.

Y

Yema.—Yolk.

Index

217

Fowl and Game

Meats

219

Pastes and Biscuits

Fruits

Cakes, Icecreams and «Turrones»